ENDORSEMENTS

Chuck and Pam Pierce make spiritual principles come alive. They are vulnerable in sharing real examples from life with a family of six children and numerous pets. What they write will speak to your heart and challenge your spirit. I recommend it!

—Joy Strang
Co-founder, Strang Communications

Thank you, Chuck and Pam, for letting us into your very real world. I honestly laughed and cried my way through this new book. Your transparency and insights will inspire all who read it. Your faith is both practical and gut honest. Twenty-first century Christians need more of this good stuff!

—Paul and Denise Goulet

In a world that sometimes feels like it's spinning out of control, faith can be hard to hold on to. In this new book, Chuck and Pam Pierce, offer hope to those whose faith is waning, strength to those whose faith needs reinforcing, and practical encouragement for *every* believer, regardless of where they are in their walk of faith. Through glimpses into their family's journey of faith, Chuck and Pam share honestly about the lessons they've learned along the way and give us practical application we can use in our everyday walk.

—Jane Hansen

From the moment I started reading the introduction, I started furiously underlining full sentences and paragraphs in this new work *One Thing*. Can you relate to this line? *"For most of us, life is composed of small moments strung together on a delicate thread in the middle of a world that appears to be out of control."* Then there's Chapter 3, *"Don't be so complex."* If you are looking for a REAL book on how YOU can live the Christian life *"in a world of chaos,"* this is the book you've been waiting for.

—Steve Shultz
THE ELIJAH LIST
www.elijahlist.com

ONE THING

HOW TO KEEP YOUR FAITH
IN A WORLD OF CHAOS

Chuck D. and Pamela J. Pierce

Destiny Image® Publishers, Inc.

P.O. Box 310
Shippensburg, PA 17257-0310

"Speaking to the Purposes of God for this Generation
and for the Generations to Come."

For Worldwide Distribution, Printed in the U.S.A.

ISBN 10: 0-7684-2379-1

ISBN 13: 978-0-7684-2379-2

This book and all other Destiny Image, Revival Press, MercyPlace, Fresh Bread, Destiny Image Fiction, and Treasure House books are available at Christian bookstores and distributors worldwide.

For a U.S. bookstore nearest you, call
1-800-722-6774.

For more information on foreign distributors, call
717-532-3040.

Or reach us on the Internet:
www.destinyimage.com

1 2 3 4 5 6 7 8 9 10 11 / 10 09 08 07 06

CONTENTS

FOREWORD

So often in the Body of Christ, when we are deeply impacted by the power and the effects of someone's ministry, we wish we could discover their secrets. Sadly, the number of ministers of the Gospel who have "let others in" on the secrets to their power and their walk of faith are few. We tend to believe that we need to guard and protect our "secrets" when it comes to the anointing. In actual fact, transparency and intimacy are the real keys to sustained power in ministry. I have been deeply impacted by Chuck Pierce over the years, and his prophetic ministry has changed my life personally on many levels. To be able to have Chuck and his wife, "let me in" on their journey through their relationship, parenting, growing together in their faith, the challenges they faced, the battles they have fought, the dreams they have dreamed together, and even the clothes they wear and why they wear them, has been both refreshing and encouraging. If there is one thing we need more than anything else in the Body of Christ in the day in which we live, it is authenticity and genuineness. To be able to get an in-depth look at how this powerful couple, who have together forged a global ministry and a family that reflects the glory of God is a gift to all who are ready to receive it. Within every one of our lives there are a number of systems in play whether we are aware of them or not. Each of those systems overlaps to affect the whole of our life and *our ministry* as well! Chuck and Pam have covered all the bases in this wonderful expression of their journey: their personal life and feelings, their life as a couple, their life as parents, their life as servants of the King, their lives as friends, and their lives as a family relating to other families. The secrets of faith, perseverance, sustainability, relentless pursuit of the will and Word of God, and the secrets of success unfold within every chapter. Their lives are an open book and what you are reading are living epistles who have fleshed out a demonstration of the Spirit's Power in the nitty-gritty, down-to-earth, human existence from which all great ministry emerges. Take the time to get to know this incredible man and woman of God (along with their children), and glean from their experience, their wisdom, and their precious faith and journey in Christ.

Here is to your transformation in God as you read!

—Dr. Mark J. Chironna
Mark Chironna Ministries
Orlando, Florida

INTRODUCTION:
CHAOS, CONFUSION, AND SIMPLE FAITH

"LIONS and tigers and bears, oh my," goes that famous line from *The Wizard of Oz*. Most of you know this classic story, especially since the movie is even more famous than the book. Dorothy, having to contend in a real world, longs for a better place, when along comes the wind that sweeps her "over the rainbow." She lands in a world controlled by a witch that she dethrones, and then the real confusion and chaos begin. The Munchkins, whom she liberates, exalt her to queenly status and make her "Queen for a Day." But like most of us, she now wants to go home—back to reality on the farm. Oh my, does that sound like most of us! We long for greener pastures, but when we get there we just want to get back to the place we left. If only the confusion and chaos of our real world would end. If we could just get out of this world and get on another path, our troubles would end.

However, after Dorothy leaves the Munchkins, she meets and teams up with the Scarecrow, who has no brain. (How many times have we met people on our path who seem to have more issues than we do?) As the two of them journey together, they discover another individual on their yellow brick road: the Tin Man. Dorothy and the Scarecrow lubricate the Tin Man's joints with oil and encourage him to join them on their journey to the Emerald City, the home of the one person who will give them the answers to their questions and meet their needs. This third person of the trio doesn't have a heart, and he wants one desperately. (Are there people now walking along with you when all you were trying to do was find your way?)

Suddenly, the other Wicked Witch appears on the cottage roof and threatens the trio. As soon as she throws a ball of fire at the Scarecrow, the witch vanishes in a cloud of red smoke. Oh my! And all Dorothy wanted was to find a peaceful place over the rainbow. (Does this sound familiar?)

The three are not deterred by the witch's threats, so they get back on the Yellow Brick Road and enter the fringes of the deep, dark forest. Their fears rise up when they see how dark and creepy the forest is, and Dorothy wonders if they will encounter wild animals. The Tin Man admits that there will probably be lions and tigers and bears. The three new friends start walking again, slowly chanting, "Lions and tigers and bears, oh my." (You know, just when we thought we were making headway the path got a little darker and our imagination kicked in and added to the mess we were already in).

Just as their momentum starts to build, one of the wild animals they fear leaps from the darkness: a lion. (Our worst fears always seem to just pop into the picture when we are already in a mess!) As Dorothy hides behind a tree, the Lion threatens the Scarecrow and the Tin Man and challenges them both to a fight. When the Lion advances on Toto, the dog (oh yes, there are always the issues with our pets that add to our confusion), Dorothy rescues him and pops the Lion on the nose. (Go girl! What do you have to lose at this point?!)

The Lion stops abruptly and starts to cry. It quickly becomes obvious that the Lion has no courage, and he decides to accompany the other three to the Emerald City in hopes that the Wizard will give him some courage. (Yes, some friends are negative and filled with fear.) The four travelers, along with Toto, continue their journey together on the Yellow Brick Road singing, "We're off to see the Wizard."

Does this sound familiar? Will we ever get to our *there*—wherever our *there* is? Like Dorothy, all we usually want is a change from the norm, peace in the midst of our confusion, and order in our chaos. We want to know that our path is leading somewhere.

The Bible is a book worth reading. I love the way the Book begins: The Spirit of God is brooding over confusion and chaos, God speaks, and a new order begins. Remember that point! We must not lose sight throughout life that there is a simple way out of our confusion and chaos.

If we will just listen, in the midst of all we are going through, He will communicate to us and open our eyes to see the higher plan. There are so many life-giving stories that help us along the road that we walk on a daily basis. And usually, all of those on our path are there for a reason.

There is a story in the Old Testament about Elijah the Prophet and one of his encounters with God. In First Kings 19, God tells Elijah, *"Go out, and stand on the mountain before the Lord."* Now Elijah has learned to do what God says over the years, so he goes out and stands on the mountain before the Lord. Before long, a strong wind tears into the mountains, but God isn't in the wind. Next, an earthquake shakes the mountain, but God isn't in the earthquake.

After the earthquake, Elijah survives a fire, but God isn't in that, either. Finally, after the wind, the earthquake, and the fire, Elijah hears God in a still, small voice.

Elijah had seen God do some amazing things during his tenure as prophet to Israel. Even so, he didn't assume that he knew how God was going to reveal Himself out on that mountain. Because of his wisdom and track record with the God of Israel, Elijah saw beyond the big demonstrations on that mountain to the heart of the matter: the still, small voice.

Elijah lived during a time of chaos and uncertainty. He had served as prophet to an apostate king, a pagan queen, and a wayward nation. He had declared the judgment of God, endured drought, escaped execution, lived in hiding, survived famine, defeated the priests of Baal, and run from a vengeful Jezebel to hide under a juniper tree. By the time he went up on that mountain to hear from God, he was a worn-out man of faith looking for some rest.

For most of us, life is composed of small moments strung together on a delicate thread in the middle of a world that appears to be out of control. Here and there along the thread we encounter the big demonstrations, but it is usually the seemingly small events that chip away or build up our character. In fact, without the small moments of preparation, those big moments would be potential land mines. The simple, everyday events fine-tune us for the milestones that everyone else sees. That's why it is so important that we recognize the value of the little stops along the way and respond in faith to God's direction.

This book is a collection of moments from our lives plucked from the chaos we all experience. Although we may not have been summoned to a mountain and waited while the wind, earthquake, and fire bombarded us, we have made our way through some treacherous places, by faith, to hear the *one thing* we needed to do or learn in the midst of confusion. We have written this book to help stir up faith in you. We are sure there have been many times when you were in a confused or chaotic state. You were attempting to stand in the midst of your confusion but didn't feel surefooted. You could feel the winds of adversity blowing hard against you. You could feel the ground shaking under you, even feel the fire of testing burn you and leave you charred. However, just in the nick of time, there was a small voice from the One who loves you most that said, "Do this and you will be at peace." We hope that after reading this book you will remember all those times when the still, small voice has spoken to you.

In this book, there will be times when the text is written from the personal perspective of Chuck or Pam, but at other times we will share from a blended perspective. Even after 33 years of marriage, we don't always see things from the same angle, nor do we always learn the same lessons through our shared experiences. This is not a book of doctrine, but a collection of experiences that have produced a firm foundation in the midst of many trials. We hope that this book will help you learn to hear and receive wisdom in a simple way in the midst of chaotic, daily activities and life trials.

Chapter 1

LETTING GO:

TRUSTING GOD TO BE AN EXCELLENT FATHER

Therefore do not worry about tomorrow,
for tomorrow will worry about its own things.
Sufficient for the day is its own trouble.
(Matthew 6:34)

IT was a crisp, clear winter day in Houston, Texas, and the sun was streaming through the bedroom window. Three-month-old Daniel slept peacefully on the bed, his wispy blond hair almost transparent in the sunlight. I sat in my rocking chair, chewing on a fingernail and worrying, again. The question just wouldn't go away. No matter what I did it just kept poking its hateful head out to taunt me. I launched myself out of the chair, tiptoed from the nursery, and picked up the telephone.

"Hello," my mother's voice answered after two rings.

Sometimes, a mother's voice is all it takes to either reassure us or send us into a fit of crying. This time, it was the latter.

"Pamela, what's wrong?"

My mother is the only one who calls me by my full name, and it always seems rather quaint and comforting. I took a deep breath to steady my voice before answering.

"It's the adoption," I said. "I'm just so afraid something will go wrong. What if we have to give Daniel back?" There, I'd asked the question out loud.

Daniel was born in October of 1981 and arrived in our home through a private adoption. I don't know how these things are handled now, but in our case the birth mother had six months to change her mind before the adoption was final. Being a bit of a pessimist, I was sure that she would do just that. After trying to get pregnant for almost eight years and finally getting a taste of motherhood, the possibility of losing this precious child was incomprehensible.

Like a lot of Christians, I had accepted a skewed version of God as an unapproachable monarch for a long time. By the time I was 28, I had begun to realize that I had believed some bad press about someone who actually loved me and wanted the absolute best for me. Even so, my mind still got in the way many times. Honestly, it was difficult for me to accept that I deserved anything good, and I lived with the fear that my happiness would be pulled out from under me any day.

"Honey, I really don't believe that is going to happen," she said in her softly reassuring voice.

"But what if it does? I'm afraid of loving him too much because it would hurt so badly to lose him," I answered lamely.

My mother was quiet for a moment. I knew she was carefully considering her next words.

"Pamela, even if the adoption goes through without a problem, you will have to live with the possibility of losing Daniel someday. So even if you only get to keep him for six months, doesn't it make more sense to love him completely for as long as you can?"

And with those words, the anxiety was gone. Just like that. It was one of those moments when—mentally, emotionally, and spiritually—faith kicked in and I knew what was true. I had been wasting precious time worrying about something that might never happen.

"Well, when you put it that way," I responded, feeling pretty stupid, "I suppose it does."

"Of course it does." I could hear the smile. "And I really believe it's going to be all right. God has a plan for Daniel's life, and He's put him right where he needs to be for his future. You just love him and take care of him."

My mother was right, of course. In April of 1982, the adoption was finalized in Harris County, Texas, and I didn't expend any more time or energy trying to protect myself from possible pain. Through the years, I have paraphrased and applied my mother's words of wisdom in countless other situations.

The peace of God had overwhelmed me, but Chuck was another matter. Most people know my husband as a modern-day giant in the faith, but he was once known as the worrier of all worriers and could have been called Mr. Anxiety. Therefore, he was experiencing his own emotional strain and crisis over the situation. He had not heard my mother's reassuring voice. Not only was his imagination working overtime, he was unsuccessfully trying to control his fear of losing this child who had come into our lives.

The next morning Chuck received a call from the social worker who was assisting us during the adoption. This was not the reassuring voice that I had heard the day before when I called my mother. Instead, she called to inform us that the presiding judge in our adoption case was known as "difficult." When Chuck got off the phone with the social worker, his face was pale (my cowardly lion) as he explained the situation.

Fortunately, by that time my faith had kicked in, and I began to lead us in prayer. If only we would remember to call out for help, wisdom, and intervention in the midst of our chaos! God began to orchestrate some interesting events. We received a call the next day informing us that the judge's mother had become ill and we were being redirected to another judge. Well, at this point, we decided to accept the unknown as a blessing.

When we arrived in court the next week, apprehensive but excited, we learned that the new judge was a University of Texas graduate. Chuck is a Texas A&M University graduate, and these two schools are long-time rivals. As soon as the judge recognized Chuck's A&M ring, the two men immediately began to good-naturedly rib each other. Our good friend, a beautiful blonde named Faye, accompanied us to the hearing. I have red hair. The judge finally just looked at Chuck and said, *"Leave the blonde and the redhead with me and you take the baby!"* The tension evaporated and faith invaded the courtroom.

That bright winter day in Houston was a turning point in our lives. It was the day we realized that love only multiplies when it's invested. We also realized the need to work together. Ecclesiastes 4:9-10 says, *"Two are better than one...for if they fall, one will lift up his companion."*

And something else changed, too. I exchanged my pessimism for faith and decided that I could, by God's grace, take one day at a time. I haven't always succeeded, but whenever I get overwhelmed by the whirlwind, the fire, and the earthquake, it usually means I have stepped back through the door of unbelief. That choice inevitably leads to fear, confusion, and acceptance of the worst possible outcome.

There are many times when the outcome is not what we hope for, but that doesn't mean it's the wrong outcome. And although we can't control the future, we can control our response to it when it comes. The fact is that bad things do happen to good people (even God's people), and bitterness only magnifies the result and leaves us vulnerable to the next assault. Knowing that I have a truly good Father enables me to take the next step regardless of my circumstances.

Children and the quest for children have always been one of the key teaching tools of my life. Two and a half years after recognizing that God is an excellent Father, I walked through a dark place that severely tested my new confidence in the goodness of God.

Daniel was a toddler by this time, full of curiosity and questions, and Chuck was on staff at a boys' home outside of Houston. In January of 1984, we attended the James Robison Bible Conference in Dallas. During a ministry time led by John Wimber, I was suddenly and sovereignly healed of barrenness. Two months later it was confirmed: I was pregnant for the first time in my life.

Reading the positive results of the pregnancy test was one of the most amazing moments in my entire life. As I held that little plastic stick in my hand, all the promises of God suddenly became more real than ever. To know beyond any doubt that God had miraculously healed me and granted my petition of ten years was life-changing. In that instant, anything was possible.

Less than two weeks later, after my first visit to the doctor, I started running a mysterious fever. Within days, the fever was accompanied by abdominal tenderness and severe neck and shoulder pain. My doctor, who was baffled and concerned, admitted me to the hospital and called in a specialist. Several blood tests later, the doctors informed us that I had contracted two viruses: Epsteins-Barr and Cytomegalovirus. The specialist kept saying, "If you weren't pregnant, there are a number of treatments we could use, but…," and the rest of us just looked at him in puzzlement.

My obstetrician, Dr. Rodriguez, explained the potential risks of cytomegalovirus on our unborn child. When he told me that our baby could have hearing loss, visual impairment, and diminished mental and motor capabilities, I was devastated. How could this be happening? Three weeks earlier, I wouldn't have believed it was possible to feel so overwhelmed and discouraged. And yet, here I was, sitting on the edge of a hospital bed, hugging a pillow, and hearing the worst news I could imagine.

It didn't take long for me to grow tired of needles, nurses, and negative reports. When I had heard enough and lost a lot more blood than I felt was necessary, I told the devil and my doctor that I was going home.

At my next office visit, Dr. Rodriguez requested that we run some tests, including an ultrasound, to determine the health of the baby.

"What if the tests show that the baby isn't healthy?" I asked. "Could you do anything about it?"

"Well, no," he admitted. "I'd just like to check because I am legally required to inform you of your options. I'm a pro-life doctor. I don't perform abortions, but I must give you the opportunity to choose."

"If it's okay with you," I said, after consulting with Chuck, "we really need to walk this out by faith. If you can't walk it out with us, then we will find another doctor."

Dr. Rodriguez looked surprised for an instant before he said, "You don't have to do that. I'll be glad to walk it out with you."

Over the next seven months, I sought God daily for some word or sign that the baby was all right. Except for one Scripture during that first week, God was silent the whole time. The only word of reassurance that I had during that time was from Job 13:15, *Though He slay me, yet will I trust Him.*" As strange as that might sound, those words sustained me until two weeks before the baby was born.

When I was two weeks from the November 4, 1984, due date, I opened up my Bible to my daily reading in the New Testament. When I reached Matthew 7:9, I knew the silence was broken: *"Or what man is there among you who, if his son asks for bread, will give him a stone?"*

That same day, Chuck brought home a new Morris Chapman album (yes, this was before compact discs). He encouraged me to listen to the album. He told me that he had felt impressed to buy it for me. Chuck loves music and has always used any excuse to buy a new album. However, I decided to stop my daily routine and listen. One of the songs contained the line, *"If you ask Him for bread, will He give you a stone?"*

This time, Chuck had been confident all along that the baby would be fine. However, it had been necessary for me to walk in the dark by faith until God broke the silence and shed His light on the situation. Two days later, during my last office visit, Dr. Rodriguez rushed me to the hospital for an emergency ultrasound because of unexplained bleeding. Even what seemed to be a great danger turned to good. After the test was completed and we saw the perfectly formed baby on the screen, my doctor flashed us a huge grin and said, "Everything's just fine."

He was right. On November 3, Rebekah Faith Pierce was born after 13 hours of labor in Tomball, Texas. Today, she is a beautiful, intelligent, creative 21-year-old who is engaged to be married. And God has proven Himself to be an excellent Father over and over again.

Chapter 2

CHAOS VERSUS SIMPLICITY:
UNDERSTANDING HOW TO FUNCTION IN FAITH

WHEN I was taking home economics in the eighth grade, one of the first things we learned to make was "simple" syrup. Unlike my early attempts at sewing in that class, the simple syrup was a success. After all, how can you mess up a recipe that tells you to combine one cup of granulated sugar and one cup of water in a saucepan and bring the mixture to a boil? Some of my classmates, however, were confused by the recipe's simplicity. One girl boiled her mixture so long that all the water evaporated and left crunchy, brown granules in the bottom of the pan. The classroom smelled like burnt cotton candy for two weeks! Another girl was so afraid that the mixture would boil over that she turned the burner down too low. She may still be standing there waiting for the syrup to thicken.

Finding simplicity in the midst of chaos is not a recipe or a formula. Instead, it is a function of faith in the believer's life. Oswald Chambers made the following observation about simplicity:

> The marvel of the grace of God is that He can take the strands of evil and twistedness out of a man's mind and imagination and make him simple towards God. Restoration through the Redemption of Jesus Christ makes a man simple, and simplicity always shows itself in action. There is nothing simple in the human soul or in human life. The only simple thing is the relationship of the soul to Jesus Christ, that is why the Apostle Paul says, "I fear, lest by any means...your minds should be corrupted from the simplicity that is in Christ."[1]

Chaos is a condition or place of great disorder or confusion; I think we all agree that the world suffers from this condition. But how often do we compound our own chaotic state by looking for complicated solutions or recipes to solve our problems? When our minds start devising routes through the chaos, we are in danger of missing the "simplicity that is in Christ."

When the Bible uses the word *simple*, it does not mean *easy*. According to *Merriam-Webster Online Dictionary*, the word *easy* means "causing or involving little difficulty or discomfort; requiring or indicating little effort, thought, or reflection." *Simple*, in the biblical sense, refers to anything that is without guile, pure, unadulterated, and free from admixture of evil.[2] Anyone who has followed the Lord Jesus Christ for more than a week can tell you that what God calls simple is not always easy!

Simple syrup is about as uncomplicated as things get in the kitchen. Those two ingredients—sugar and water—when combined in the proper amounts under the right conditions, become the basis for a myriad of other applications. As deep and mysterious as the Word of God can be to understand sometimes, the underlying simplicity of Christ serves to anchor our hearts in the midst of life's storms. It is the basis for every application with which we are faced in this life.

I can think of hundreds of examples of this principle from my own past, but I want to share one testimony that continually reminds me of the foolishness of man compared with the wisdom of God.

Simple Obedience

I shared with you a portion of the story of having my first pregnancy, which produced Rebekah Faith Pierce. There was so much trial to bring forth this child. The trial actually began long before she was conceived. Many of you have heard Chuck on his speaking tours share our testimony about my being barren. Let me share with you what it was like from the beginning.

I was plagued with the thought that there had to be something wrong with me; otherwise, why would a healthy, 20-something-year-old woman be unable to get pregnant? I ate right, I exercised daily, my cycle was regular, yet after seven years of marriage I still could not conceive a child. My husband and I were faithful members of our local church, and I thought we were serving the Lord. All of our married friends had one or two children already, and I could feel their pity every year when Mother's Day rolled around again.

It didn't help when I read Psalm 127:3: "*Behold, children are a heritage from the Lord, the fruit of the womb is a reward."* Reward for what? Was there something I was missing, something I was supposed to be doing in order to receive the reward of children? It also didn't help when well-meaning friends assured me that the Lord had already given me "spiritual children" through the young people we mentored in our home. As much as I loved those teenagers, I still felt defective because of my barrenness.

I wanted answers, so I went to a fertility specialist in Houston. After running a series of tests, the verdict was returned: I had endometriosis, and conception would be impossible without intensive drug therapy and/or surgery. This didn't seem like a simple solution to my problem.

I had a decision to make. One friend asked why I didn't get started on the drugs right away. Another one assumed that I would schedule the surgery immediately. But I wasn't so sure. The solution seemed obvious enough, but my mind was in complete chaos. You see, as soon as the doctor presented me with the options and assured me that I would be able to get pregnant within a year of treatment, I was petrified.

I'm not embarrassed to admit that the word *surgery* makes me really nervous, and taking anything stronger than over-the-counter pain reliever is a huge step for me. But this was a different kind of fear. *It was the fear of artificially altering God's plan for my life.*

Although I had never hesitated to seek a doctor's help in the past when I was sick, this was somehow different. With hope of a cure in plain sight, I was afraid of changing something that God was using to keep me in His perfect timing.

I couldn't do it. A friend of mine who had gone through the surgery for endometriosis and now had a beautiful baby boy asked me about my decision. All I could say was that until I was absolutely certain it was the right thing for me, I was going to wait on the Lord just a little bit longer.

So I did. I waited, and during the next year an amazing thing happened: God became so real and present in my life that my barrenness didn't matter anymore. For the first time, I could say with complete conviction that if I never had a child, God was enough. The feelings of inadequacy and emptiness simply dissipated. In their place was a sense of wholeness I never could have imagined!

By the end of the year we had adopted Daniel. Of course, had I been pregnant at the time of Daniel's conception, we would never have been considered as candidates to adopt him. What a blessing we would have missed had I barreled headlong into treatments for barrenness! I felt humbled and rewarded all at one time. It just couldn't get any better!

Then God spoke. Daniel was asleep in his crib. I was reading my Bible in the next room when a phrase from First Timothy 5:14 jumped off the page: "*...that the younger women marry, **bear children**...*" (KJV). Regardless of the context, God was plainly saying that He wanted me to bear children in addition to adopting.

At first I didn't know what to do with this information. Then God led me to a passage in First Samuel 1:9-17:

So Hannah arose after they had finished eating and drinking in Shiloh. Now Eli the priest was sitting on the seat by the doorpost of the tabernacle of the Lord. And she was in bitterness of soul, and prayed to the Lord and wept in anguish. Then she made a vow and said, "O Lord of hosts, if You will indeed look on the affliction of Your maidservant and remember me, and not forget

Your maidservant, but will give Your maidservant a male child, then I will give him to the Lord all the days of his life, and no razor shall come upon his head." And it happened, as she continued praying before the Lord, that Eli watched her mouth. Now Hannah spoke in her heart; only her lips moved, but her voice was not heard. Therefore Eli thought she was drunk. So Eli said to her, "How long will you be drunk? Put your wine away from you!" But Hannah answered and said, "No, my lord, I am a woman of sorrowful spirit. I have drunk neither wine nor intoxicating drink, but have poured out my soul before the Lord. Do not consider your maidservant a wicked woman, for out of the abundance of my complaint and grief I have spoken until now." Then Eli answered and said, "Go in peace, and the God of Israel grant your petition which you have asked of Him."

The moment I finished reading that passage, I knew what I had to do. I picked up the telephone and called my pastor. I knew I had to act quickly, before my mind had the opportunity to reason away this course of action. That afternoon, I went to the church office to meet with Brother Billy. I didn't waste any time with pleasantries when he asked how I was doing. I explained to him what God had shown me in First Timothy and First Samuel.

"It's simple," I finished. "You are supposed to agree with me in prayer just like Eli did when Hannah poured her heart out to God."

This precious man of God never questioned the directive or doubted my faith. He immediately knelt down next to me, placed his hand on my shoulder, and repeated Eli's words to Hannah: "Go in peace, Pam, and the God of Israel grant your petition which you have asked of Him."

Okay, that wasn't too hard, I thought. But that wasn't all! *As soon as I left the church office, the Lord told me to start operating as though faith was already sight.* For the next several months, God gave me countless opportunities to share what was happening in my life. I was sure that some people thought I was delusional when I declared my healing with such strong confidence. At this time in our lives, we were worshiping in a traditional, denominational church, so declaring one's faith for healing was unusual. Most of the time, God's simple solution was easy, but there were many times when I felt like a fool.

I even dressed for the occasion. My mother-in-law, a wonderful, pragmatic lady (my Naomi) who worked at Dillard's department store in another Texas city, decided to send me a gift for no occasion. I called her to thank her when I received the new dress she sent, and she promptly said, "They are the latest thing in the store." This dress, which I still have to this day, was a red, floral print, baby doll dress. For you who do not remember, these dresses were loose—very loose! They had large white collars and hung without touching the body anywhere. *This was not a maternity dress, but one that appeared to be a dress for someone pregnant.* They were the style of the season—my season of faith.

I was invited to a local Christian garden club luncheon the next week and wore my "faith dress." The first question the hostess asked me was, "When is the baby due?" I answered by faith, "Soon," and launched into my testimony. The hostess was so blessed by the way God was working in my life that she asked me to share the story with the rest of the women. This was a major step for me. I was definitely on a faith journey, and God wanted me dressed for the road ahead!

Just a few days before my healing was manifested at the 1984 James Robison Bible Conference in Dallas, Texas, the enemy came in like a flood. Our staff house at Boy's Country of Houston had flooded, and we had been living in one of the other cottages on campus. Houston was in the grips of one of the worst cold spells in its history. The prospect of cleaning, replacing carpet, and repairing sheetrock was overwhelming me. I was losing sight of the goodness of God and wondering if I had really heard God say I was to "bear children."

As Chuck, Daniel, and I drove from Houston to Dallas early in January 1984, I was in a depressed and discouraged state of mind. We got into a debate about the value of "raising hands" in worship. At this time, we were still members of an evangelical, denominational church that didn't endorse charismatic worship practices. I recognized later that the enemy was trying to distract me from what God was about to do, but as we drove along the interstate highway I just wanted to pick a fight. I told Chuck (who was constantly creating a stir by raising his hands in church when a powerful declaration occurred or song came forth) that the New Testament only referred to raising hands twice.

"Honey, I don't care how many times the Bible tells us to 'lift holy hands' when we worship," Chuck finally said in exasperation. "If it only said it one time it would be enough for me to raise my hands and worship Jesus! And furthermore, I could care less if it is in the concordance! You get desperate enough in all of your circumstances and you will raise your hands, stand on your head, or do whatever, to sense the Lord's presence." (Chuck had experienced some very desperate times in his life and the Lord had met him during those times. You will read about some of this in a later chapter.)

That did it. As soon as those words left Chuck's mouth, the Holy Spirit broke through my last piece of defensive stubbornness. I released an old mind-set just in time. At the Bible conference the very next day, the sovereign Hand of God touched me. Chuck shares the situation this way:

"I felt the Lord's presence very strongly during the time when John Wimber was ministering to pregnant women. At first I was afraid that Pam would be pulled back into a place of despair over her barrenness. However, when I turned to look at her, she had both hands lifted high and tears were running down her cheeks. 'What is happening?' I asked; to which she replied, 'The Lord is healing me of my barrenness.'"

I was standing in the middle of a crowd, hands raised in worship, when I felt the warmth of God's healing power engulf me from head to toe. One month later, after the first normal menstrual period of my adult life, I was pregnant with our daughter, Rebekah Faith.

Chuck always says, "The Lord was just waiting for you to praise and express your love to Him in a new way. He then poured His power into you and unlocked that which would have kept our seeds from coming forth!"

In the midst of chaos—barrenness—God revealed one simple thing: faithful obedience. Although it wasn't always easy to follow God's simple solution, the journey was worth it because it led to a new place of communion and revelation. Let me share some insight from Oswald Chambers on obedience:

No one can tell us where the shadow of the Almighty is, we have to find it out for ourselves. When by obedience we have discovered where it is, we must abide there—"there shall no evil befall thee, neither shall any plague come nigh thy dwelling." That is the life that is more than a conqueror because the joy of the Lord has become its strength, and that soul is on the way to entering ultimately into the joy of the Lord.[3]

Obedience to the will and the Word of God leads into the shadow of the Almighty. No matter how chaotic our surroundings, we can enter that abiding place and find refuge and strength in the joy of the Lord.

Finding the Way Home

Have you ever noticed how many books, movies, songs, and poems are about finding the way home? In the *Wizard of Oz*, Dorothy was desperate to find her way home from the confusing land over the rainbow. She thought she wanted adventure, but running from a witch in a world full of talking trees, scarecrows, and animals was making Kansas look better all the time! Dorothy and her companions endured danger and hardship, forged new friendships, fulfilled the wizard's requirements, and overcame evil. Finally, after the Scarecrow, Tin Man, and Cowardly Lion received their gifts from the wizard, it was Dorothy's turn. But Dorothy's way back to Kansas had been right under her nose all along—or rather, right on her feet. With a click of her heels and a wish in her heart, the ruby slippers returned Dorothy to her black-and-white Kansas bedroom. Simple, but not easy!

Sometimes animals are so much wiser than we are. About a year ago, our middle son, John, moved into a house four blocks away from ours. He took with him our golden retriever-mix dog, Casey. Casey is a big, fluffy, lovable animal that we adopted from the Colorado Springs SPCA in September 1999. The only bad habit that Casey has is his tendency to run off when he manages to escape through an opened gate or front door. He always comes home about 30 minutes later, out of breath and lathering at the mouth, and collapses on the cool tile of the kitchen floor.

I made certain that Casey was secure in John's backyard before I let him move into the new place. There were two pet doors leading from the utility room, into the garage, then into the backyard so Casey would be free to go in and out as he pleased. John and his roommates bought the dog a big box of milk bones and proceeded to spoil him rotten with attention.

It appeared that Casey had made the adjustment to his new environment with no problem until the first time he escaped through the front door. Within ten minutes, Casey had found his way back to my door and was barking excitedly. I let him in and followed him to the pantry, where he danced around in anticipation of a dog biscuit. As soon as he was settled on the kitchen floor with his treat, I called John.

"Where's Casey?" I asked innocently.

"Uh-mmm," John began, "he pushed open the storm door and got out of the house. How'd you know? Have you seen him?"

"He's in my kitchen, eating a milk bone," I answered. "He knows his way home."

Since that day, whenever Casey escapes from John's house, I get a call from John or one of his roommates.

"Be on the lookout for Casey," they will say. And, sure enough, Casey will arrive within ten minutes, ready for a treat and a romp with the other dogs in the household.

I'm sure that Casey will one day see John's house as his home; but in the meantime, I'm glad he remembers his way back to my door. It may take a while before the old pattern of returning to this place can be replaced with a new pattern leading to John's door.

In the same way, we have to learn new patterns throughout our lives: new ways of thinking, believing, seeing, and receiving. These new patterns—transformations—are moving us closer and closer to new abiding places in the Lord. As we respond to the simplicity that is in Christ, we are one step closer to our restoration, and worlds away from the chaos.

Endnotes

1. Oswald Chambers, *Oswald Chambers: The Best From All His Books* (Nashville, TN: Thomas Nelson, 1987), 323.

2. *Vine's Expository Dictionary of Biblical Words* (Thomas Nelson Publishers, 1985).

3. Oswald Chambers, *Oswald Chambers: The Best From All His Books* (Nashville, TN: Thomas Nelson, 1987), 227.

Chapter 3

DON'T BE SO COMPLEX!

JUST DO THE ONE THING HE TELLS YOU

A S you read in the previous chapter, while Pam was sick during her pregnancy with Rebekah, I was experiencing a different dimension in faith. I want to explain how I operate in the midst of very confused circumstances.

The world can be complex. However, the things of the world and the systems and structures around us are, perhaps, not true reality. Many things around us exist to conform us into a way of thinking that negates simple faith and action. Reality is something not imagined or pretended, but the quality of something being true to life. Reality is more than just fact. Reality is where you actually experience *LIFE* as defined by the Life Giver.

My family many times asks me to go to the movies with them. Pam, however, knows what movies can send me over the edge. Therefore, she is a little more cautious before she recommends something. I am sensitive to things around me, so some movies, no matter how innocent, can send me flying into a spiritual pandemonium.

Jurassic Park, a movie about recreating dinosaurs through DNA manipulation and placing them in an amusement park, is a good example. This movie, based on the book by Michael Crichton and directed by Steven Spielberg, was one of my family's favorites. I was not bold enough to watch the movie on the "big screen." After it was available on video, I gave it a shot on one of our family nights. When the T-Rex ate the goat, I was screaming and yelling. Isaac, seven years old at the time, looked up from the floor and promptly said, "Dad, this is one of my favorite parts. If you can't handle it, you need to go to your room." This gives you an idea of how my vivid imagination can sometimes get the best of me.

Then there was *The Matrix*. This movie was a blockbuster. Most people I know went to see it. Most people found all the spiritual implications in it. Many suggested that I go. My first thought was this: Well, *matrix* is a biblical word. When the Lord knit us together in our mother's womb, the Bible says He matrixed us and knew everything about us. Matrix is linked with mother and means that from which we are formed, where our casting, shaping, impressions, and inner cellular substance is developed.

I asked Pam about the movie, and she insisted that I go with two of the kids. I know she assumed that if I went with Rebekah and Isaac, I would probably be fine. After yelling inside the movie theater (causing my kids to move to the other side of the theater so they would not be associated with me), I walked out, went to the lobby, and called home. I needed my wife to explain what was going on in this movie that she had recommended. (In fact, I actually called home five times during the show.) She explained the movie the following way:

"The writers created a world dominated by machines in which humans were valued only as a source of energy. When the protagonist, Neo, discovered that the world he accepted as real was, in fact, a computer-generated hoax perpetuated by artificial intelligence, he had to choose between the *red pill* and the *blue pill*. If Neo chose the blue pill, he could return to his phony (but safe) life and never be the wiser. If, however, Neo chose the red pill, he would be expelled from the human battery factory and enter the difficult life of true reality. *He chose the red pill.* The red pill initiated Neo into a world of harsh struggle in which the humans waged constant war with the machines. The machines only valued humans as a power source, and they maintained the illusion created by the matrix in order to lull the human mind into acceptance."

When the movie, *The Matrix*, was released in 1999, it raised the bar for future science fiction films because of its technical and creative qualities. David Dark says this:

> With the latest *New York Times* in one hand and a Bible (NRSV) in the other, we try to explain ourselves to ourselves. What compels me? How did these clichés manage to hijack my consciousness? What does it profit a person to gain all the homeland security in the world and forfeit his soul? What is the Matrix? Or, to borrow a line from Elvis Costello's "Green Shirt": "Who put these fingerprints on my imagination?" What man, mind, or monster did (is doing) this? When and how did our thoughts get to feeling like they're not entirely our own? And when did we agree to it? Who benefits from our sedation?

Who colonized my brain space? How hard it is to prefer the pounding headache of looking hard at the world over the blissful, happy-ending incomprehensibility of Technicolor and the easy answer, simple explanation, sound-bite culture of *Fox News Network*.[1]

He goes on to say:

As a high school English teacher in America, ever in desperate need of a difficult-to-contest analogy, I've found a very present help in the metaphorical value, maximum applicability, and effective citation afforded by *The Matrix*. While very few propositions go unchallenged in a good classroom discussion, the intense relevance of this film to the experience of your average American teenager is something of a no-brainer. My students often accuse me of madness, but they find nothing particularly controversial in my observation that *The Matrix* powerfully names and describes the forms of captivity into which we're born and within which we live and move and, by all appearances, have our being. They know that worlds have been constructed around them, physically and psychologically, as protection against many a perceived threat, and they understand that it is an effort, oftentimes well-intentioned and always in progress. They also understand that they are a target market whose buying power sustains the economy and that enormous amounts of money, mind-power, and resources are expended anticipating and manipulating their desires. They live with the notion that their speech and their way of looking at the world are often the creation of television and market research....[2]

Let's look at another way of grabbing hold of reality: *In a world of chaos, do not miss the simple things*. Those "simple things" are what usually show us true value. They create a faith dimension that we can touch. They even have us touch eternity, which is reality. Young people understand the concept of this red pill. I actually think most of us are searching for reality. I also believe that only by touching the ONE who created reality can we find and distinguish between what is real or detrimental to us in the long run.

Let's get back to the first pregnancy and the situation with Rebekah. This was a time of hard circumstances trying to overwhelm our life. I had changed our assignment and moved from being on a church staff to serving at a Boys and Girls Home. There were 100 young people who had problems, a staff with problems, and an organization that seemed to have problems. On top of this, our long-awaited promise of bearing a child had become a reality, yet now we were hearing about all these health problems that could happen to the child as she was knit together in Pam's womb. Additionally, there were financial problems. I was in a walk of faith over finances. We had received a notice from the IRS that I owed some money after leaving my secular job, and we had doctor bills, and so on. And on top of this, Pam had lost the use of her left arm during her sickness. I'm telling you—it was a mess!

One night I felt overwhelmed by the world's circumstances. I made a list of everything that was overwhelming me. I looked at the list that had seven major categories and felt totally overwhelmed. I laid the list aside and went ahead and completed the next day's duties and issues. Later that night I could not rest. Therefore, after Pam went to bed, I took my list and went outside in the field and sat before the Lord.

Prayer can take different forms. I knew that the only way I could make it through all of these issues was for the Lord to somehow intervene in my life. I held the list up to the Lord and said, "Read this list!" I knew the Lord understood all the issues on the list, but it was like I just needed Him to see what was bombarding me at this point.

I am sure some of you reading this have felt this way. I then said to the Lord, "What is it that You would have me do with all of this?" And I sat there. By this time, it was around 11:30 P.M. and I wondered if I was going to sit out in the field all night. A few moments later I felt a very clear impression. I heard that wonderful voice say, "Buy your wife a new dress." Now, I only had $67 in our bank account. But I knew His voice.

This was the Thursday before Easter. I knew I was not working on Friday, so I took my list and wrote at the bottom of it what the Lord had asked me to do.

The next morning I told Pam that we were going to go shopping to buy her a new dress. She questioned me for a moment, but then I said, "It's just what we are supposed to do." We went and bought a new dress, on sale. We then had lunch at a cafeteria and came home. I had two dollars left. Therefore, when the offering plate was passed on Sunday, I just threw those two dollars into the plate and said, "Lord, me and my list are now Yours."

It was amazing what happened next. I looked up in the midst of the choir where my wife sang. While the preacher was preaching, I saw someone throw their hand up in the air. It was Pam! This was not a place that you would have thought a person would be having a spiritual experience of overwhelming praise. The message was not that moving. In fact, it was sort of boggy. On the way home after church I said to Pam, "What were you doing throwing your hand up in the midst of that awful sermon?" (Biblically, the Bible tells us to raise our hands and praise the Lord.) I did not see any reason for praise.

Pam said to me, "During the service I reached down to pull up my pantyhose and the Spirit of God touched me and healed my arm!" THIS WAS ON MY LIST! She continued, "I could do nothing but throw my arm up!"

I countered, "But the message was so awful. The pastor was even sharing how healing was not in the atonement."

She promptly said, "I am sure glad that God didn't listen to his message."

The Lord had read my list and heard my prayer. Within the next six months, EVERYTHING ON THE LIST was taken care of. All it took was for me to do the one thing the Lord asked me to do: *buy my wife a new dress.*

Faith requires action. What we see by faith is reality. Usually, the complicated things around us are binding us to a wrong thought process.

This is how Jesus began His earthly ministry. In John 2, we find Jesus and His disciples attending a wedding with His mother. During the wedding celebration (which customarily lasted seven days), they had run out of wine. His mother operated in the principle that I just described to you. She first asked our Lord to do something. Initially, He seemed reluctant to act. She then told the guests to "do whatever He tells you to do."

Of course, you know the story. He tells them to bring water pots, which represented their ritualistic purification rites, and to fill them full of water. He then changes the water into wine. The wine at the end is better than the wine at the beginning. He does this to show us that all of our ritualistic, religious perceptions can be changed by one touch from Him. He also does this to begin a manifestation of His glory to those following Him. He even says that this incident will cause them to believe.

Belief is linked with faith, which is linked with glory, which is linked with reality. In the Western world, we really do not see the Glory Realm as reality. We can only access this realm by faith. Faith takes action from us—some sort of response.

Faith takes us doing that "ONE THING" He requires of us.

Concerning the movie, *The Matrix*, Dark concludes, "But there is something powerfully invigorating about imagining, especially in the company of young people, what it might mean to take the *red pill of reality* on a regular basis or to weather the storm to the limits of one's bubble and to break on through to the other side." [3]

Let me say it this way: "All it really takes is performing one simple faith action to experience reality, and all of the complexities of the world around you begin to dissipate." I am not going to tell you to take the red pill, but I am going to tell you, "Get still, present your list of problems to the Lord, and do the one thing He tells you to do. Then you will see a manifestation of His reality."

Because I travel the world, serve on many ministry boards, assist in raising six kids, work full time for two ministries, and serve as the set leader of the church I attend, my life could seem complex. However, I have learned this "One Thing Principle." Without it, life would be overwhelming. I would lose sight of what is real. My circumstances from any of the above areas would probably bring confusion into my life.

With all the complexities of the world around us, any of us could end up like Martha of Bethany in Luke 10. Martha was preoccupied with work and too busy to sit and listen to what the Lord was teaching. Mary, on the other hand, dropped everything and seated herself at the Lord's feet. Martha even got angry because Mary would not assist her in serving. Martha was distracted by serving. The word *distracted* means "dragging around in circles." Martha even made a demand on the Lord to make Mary come "drag around in circles" with her. I like to insert my own name in the Lord's reply: *"Chuck, Chuck, you are anxious and troubled about many things. There is need of only ONE...Mary has chosen the good portion, that which is to her advantage which shall not be taken away from her"* (see Luke 10:41-42).

I try to recognize when my emotions mirror those of Martha's. Through the years, I have been learning to resist the power of anxiety that would overwhelm me, capture my imagination, and confuse me with a skewed reality of what is truly important. We must all remember to do the ONE THING.

Endnotes

1. David Dark, "Who Put These Fingerprints on My Imagination," adapted from *Everyday Apocalypse*, (Brazos Press, 2003).

2. Ibid.

3. Ibid.

Chapter 4

LOST AND FOUND:
RECOVERING HIDDEN TREASURES

*"I will give you the treasures of darkness
and hidden riches of secret places...."*
(Isaiah 45:3)

WHOEVER coined the term "youth retreat" was either not in his right mind or had never been with a group of young people on a bus. In my experience as a mother and a youth ministry worker, the only time youth *retreat* is when they go to sleep (usually well after midnight). With that knowledge realistically tucked away, I volunteered to accompany our church youth group on a "retreat" to the Texas Hill Country in the summer of 2003. A handful of college-aged and older adults would be driving for about six hours, one way, with approximately 40 teenagers from Denton to Kerrville, Texas, where we would spend two days along the Guadalupe River at Kerrville-Schreiner Park.

Just north of Waco the caravan stopped in West, Texas, to fill up with gas and freshly baked Czech pastries. Then it was on to Pedernales (pronounced Purr-DIN-alice by native

Texans) Falls State Park for a picnic lunch and energy-expending activities along the river.

Pedernales Falls State Park, 32 miles west of Austin, is a 4,800-acre park where eight miles of the flint-strewn Pedernales River meander through the limestone Hill Country of the Edward's Plateau. We picnicked near the Falls, a stretch of the river where water drops 50 feet over successive limestone layers via a series of cascades and pools. One of the adult volunteers had planned several "Survivor" challenges for the youth group teams, which involved plenty of running and sweating. By the time we loaded everyone back into the vans, tired and re-hydrated, they were ready to finish the last leg of our trip to Kerrville.

As we unloaded supplies into the group cabin in Kerrville, my 14-year-old son, Isaac, found me in the kitchen.

"I can't find my wallet," he said. "It had my money, my friend's money, my ID, my Six Flags season pass...." By this time, he was talking much faster than usual and looking a little frantic.

"Okay, okay," I said, in my most soothing mother voice. "When do you remember having it last?"

"At the river, when we were playing in the water after lunch," he said with certainty. "I put it inside my shoes on a rock."

I looked at his feet. The shoes were there.

"Have you checked the van and your backpack?" I asked, already knowing the answer.

Isaac rolled his eyes and said, "It's not here anywhere. I know I left it at Pedernales. It must have fallen in the water when I picked up my shoes."

"Well, we can't go back and get it," I said, anticipating his next idea. "If it fell in the river, we won't be able to find it in the dark. All we can do is pray and ask the Lord to let a park ranger find it. When that happens, your ID has your name and address on it, and you'll get it back."

Isaac looked skeptical, but he agreed to pray about it. We put that concern aside and had a wonderful time.

Chuck was on one of his many trips while we were in the Hill Country. (I think he had conveniently planned this one so he would not have to "rough it" with me and the youth.) However, upon his return he wanted to know all the details of the trip. As I was telling him that the trip was wonderful and we had no major issues, Isaac walked into the kitchen. That's when I remembered the wallet incident. (I had done so many things since then I had actually forgotten that crisis). I said, "Isaac, tell Dad what happened to you."

Isaac proceeded to tell his dad about his loss. By this time, he had recovered from the shock. Knowing that his dad is a good father, he concluded by saying, "And Dad, my money was in there and my Six Flags season pass. You need to replace these because I want to go to Six Flags next week."

Chuck is usually an easier mark than I am where the kids are concerned. However, he immediately said, "I could do that, but I'm not going to. We will just have to pray and ask the Lord to find the wallet if you want to go to Six Flags again."

Chuck remembers the next part of the story this way:

Isaac and I went to his room and we got down to pray. By this time, I really had lost that burst of faith and moment of grandeur that had occurred in the kitchen. However, since I am older and more spiritual, I told Isaac that I would pray first, then he could pray. I prayed a quick prayer, then waited for Isaac to pray. He proceeded by saying, "Lord, You are just going to have to help me find that wallet I lost in the river. It is red with a Volcom emblem on it. And Lord, I have asked my Dad and He will not help me!"

Now usually, in the midst of prayer, I do not want to choke someone, but my thought was, "Why am I getting the blame over his mistake?"

Isaac continued to pray, "You know, Lord, I feel that You want me to go to Six Flags, so please help me since Dad isn't. Amen!" I just looked at him and left the room, certain that we would never see the wallet again and that somehow I was now branded as a crummy dad.

On my next trip to Minnesota, as I was speaking in front of a large group of people, my cell phone rang. I had forgotten to turn it off before the message. I noticed that it was "Home," so I answered it from the pulpit. It was an excited Isaac. He said, "Dad, the park ranger found my wallet in the river! Can you believe that?"

I was in the pulpit, so I did not want to lie. I said, "No, that is hard to believe." He then proceeded without a breath by asking, "Now, when are we going to Six Flags?"

After Chuck left the pulpit in Minnesota, he called home for details. That morning, before Isaac woke up, I had received a call from a park ranger at Pedernales Falls.

"Does Isaac Pierce live there?" he asked.

"Yes, sir; I'm his mother."

"Is he by any chance missing a red, Velcro wallet?"

"As a matter of fact, he is," I answered. "Our youth group stopped at Pedernales on the way to Kerrville. Isaac was sure he lost it in the river. It contained some money, his ID, and a Six Flags season pass."

"Sounds about right," the ranger responded. "I don't know how much money he had when he lost the wallet, but there's about $50 here. If the address on the ID is correct, I'll drop this in the mail tomorrow."

After confirming the address, I had just one question.

"Could you tell me where the wallet was found?"

"One of our rangers found it just downstream from the Falls, wedged between some rocks. A bright red wallet kind of stands out in the river, you know."

I hung up the phone and turned to my 16-year-old son, John, who had been listening to my side of the conversation.

"You want to go tell Isaac they found his wallet?" I said.

"Dude, no way!" said John excitedly, rushing to Isaac's bedroom with the news.

Moments later, Isaac stumbled to the kitchen, rubbing the sleep from his eyes.

"They found my wallet?" he asked, groggy and disbelieving.

"A park ranger found it in the river, just downstream from the Falls," I said. "They're putting it in the mail tomorrow."

"I never thought…" Isaac started. "Was everything still in it?"

"Everything, including the money," I said. "You want to call Dad?"

The unexpected restoration of lost possessions is an amazing feeling. Even though Isaac and I had prayed for the wallet's return, we were both surprised by the ranger's telephone call. Chuck was overcome by the return. When the wallet arrived a few days later, still full of money, ID, season pass, and damp movie ticket stubs, it was much more than a wallet to Isaac and to us.

It was a miracle!

Expecting the miraculous is one of the childlike characteristics that has to be cultivated and protected in a world full of cynicism and disappointment. Whether the miracle comes in the form of a water-logged wallet or a restored inheritance makes no difference.

In my case, the lost item was a collection of old black-and-white photographs in a plastic pencil pouch. My early childhood was not exactly idyllic, but I didn't really pay that much attention to how dysfunctional things were around our house. In fact, by the time we moved from California to Houston, Texas, in 1964, I had grown accustomed to lots of freedom and very little parental involvement. My sister and I learned to navigate our way around the city by bus with our two best friends, Vicki and Terri. I was the official photographer and documented all of our adventures with my trusty Instamatic camera. By the time my sister and I left Texas in 1964 to live with our aunt and uncle in New Hampshire, I had a plastic pencil pouch full of black-and-white memories to take with me.

Over the years, I added a few special photographs to the pouch. Eventually, some color began to appear in the photographs, but most of them were still black-and-white. When I got married and moved into an apartment at Texas A&M University in College Station, the pouch went with me. When my husband, Chuck, graduated and accepted a job in Houston, I put a bank check bearing our College Station address in the pouch as a souvenir of our first residence as a married couple. Then I slipped the pouch in the last box, loaded it into Chuck's uncle's truck, and we were off to a new life.

Unpacking is much more fun than packing, especially when you don't own very much. Within a few days, all of our worldly possessions were stowed in our new apartment, with one glaring exception: the plastic pencil pouch of photographs. I went back through every box and every scrap of packing paper, but no matter where or how thoroughly I searched, I couldn't find it. The photographs were gone. Somewhere between College Station and Houston, my pouch full of memories had been lost.

For the next 13 years I kept expecting to find those pictures every time we moved into a new house. Surely I had just overlooked the pouch somewhere along the way and they would turn up the next time I unpacked. Everything else in that last box packed in College Station survived the trip. Why not the photographs?

Meanwhile, our family of two had turned into a family of six. By March of 1988, we were living in a little gray house on a hill in Denton, Texas. Winter was fading slowly and spring was fighting valiantly to take its rightful place, but it was a hard battle that year in many ways. In February, we had lost identical twin boys shortly after birth. Within a few weeks of their deaths, we received news that a friend of ours had died with AIDS. A week later, the kids' favorite goldfish was discovered floating, belly up, on the surface of the aquarium after a visiting child scraped most of the scales from his body. Then, to finish off the month of March, pill bugs chewed up every petunia I had planted in the garden overnight. Sometimes, when it rains it really does pour. I just sat down in the yard and had a good cry over everything.

That afternoon, when I walked to the street to pick up the mail, there was a manila envelope in the mailbox bearing a College Station post office stamp. The name in the return address field was Pierce, but I was sure we didn't know any Pierces in College Station. The envelope was addressed to Mr. and Mrs. Charles Pierce, so I sat down on the front steps and opened it. Inside was a white envelope addressed to C. Pierce of Bryan, Texas, from someone named Horne in Marshall, Texas. Along with the white envelope was a slip of yellow paper containing this message:

Dear Mr. & Mrs. Pierce,

These pictures were found in a truck belonging to a Mr. Horne and mailed to me by mistake thinking I was Charles Pierce. I then called the Former Students' Association and got your address in Denton—I do truly hope these are yours!

C. Pierce

The bank check bearing our address in College Station was folded inside the slip of yellow paper. My hands shook as I tilted the white envelope and watched my dog-eared collection of photographs spill into my lap.

Timing is everything. The pouch full of photographs had escaped the moving box in 1975 and fallen, unnoticed, behind the truck seat. For years those pictures had lain hidden, but safe, while the truck changed owners. Finally, when the time was right, someone named Horne decided to seriously clean out his truck. Mr. Horne could have taken one look at that packet of photographs and tossed them in the trash can, but he didn't. He pursued the only lead he had: an old bank check from College Station, Texas. When C. Pierce in Bryan, Texas, received the packet of photographs, she took the time to track down the current address of a former Texas A&M Aggie named Charles Pierce. She repacked the envelope containing the photographs and the bank check and sent them on the last leg of the journey so that the package arrived just in time.

I had to buy a new pencil pouch at Wal-Mart to replace the old one, but those photographs have been in my underwear drawer ever since. That seemed like the best place to put them, since I would see the pencil pouch every day. Those recovered photos are a constant, tangible reminder of one very important fact: God knows where I am and just what I need at all times. Expect the miraculous. His timing is perfect.

Chapter 5

OUT OF THE MOUTH OF BABES:

HOW FAITH CAN BECOME SIMPLE

Now you can see our philosophy on faith. Usually it is one simple act of obedience that creates a faith connection with the Creator of the universe. Wow—what a statement that is! But really, that's how simple it is. When we think of salvation or saving grace, sometimes it's such a huge mystery that we can't grab hold of the concept. However, when we see that we have been created, or *matrixed*, in our mother's womb for a purpose, then there is some drive within us that is always trying to see the "big picture." The big picture can be way too complex at times. This big picture is more like a jigsaw puzzle. We're getting a piece here and a piece there, and finally things fall into place and we see that there is a vision for our life.

However, in the midst of all the puzzle pieces we lose sight of the purpose, get confused, and become dependent upon ourselves to put it all together. Before long we just say, "Who are we and where are we going?"

Faith is relational. As a matter of fact, we'd better define *faith* since the purpose of this book is to release faith and joy within you. The Bible says *"that faith comes by hearing and hearing by the word of the Lord."* Faith comes! We also find one of the Old Testament prophets saying, *"The just shall live by faith."*

I have actually written a whole book with Robert Heidler on faith. That book is called *Restoring Your Shield of Faith* (Regal Books, 2003), and we wrote it because the Bible says that the shield of faith can quench all the fiery darts of the enemy. I am a warrior! And as a warrior, I want to quench the fiery darts of the enemy; therefore I must be sure that I understand faith. Rather than explaining all of the faith concepts here, I would encourage you to read *Restoring Your Shield of Faith*.

What I do want to explain is the importance of *hearing*. It seems that the more complex our life gets, the less we hear what we need to hear. Since faith comes by hearing what God is saying to us, the devil must want to stop a person from hearing.

A good way of thinking about faith is as a helpless child needing to be nourished. You ask for what you need, you hear what you need to hear, and then you receive that for which you have asked. That is why we find faith expressed as a childlike reliance on the words of God to lead and guide us into life. Faith is not intellectual. You have to believe that the Lord *SIMPLY* exists. Psalm 8:2 says, *"Out of the mouth of babes and unweaned infants you have established strength (praise) because of your foes, that you might silence the enemy and the avenger."*

Faith is actually a substance. It's not invisible, nor is it blind. Faith is where we personally develop a relationship with a person who helps us to hear, observe, and see the best for our lives. Our faith comes when we commit to this relationship. True faith is linked with the action resulting from this commitment. It's not just believing in a person, but intimately believing the person.

In a complex world we lose our childlike faith. Usually, it's because we are competing to "win" in the world system. However, God can restore our childlike faith. We are writing to all the various facets of society's complexities. Some of you are in the education system, some of you are dealing with huge economic decisions, and then some of you are even called to the government or political realm. Let's just remember that wherever we are, it is childlike faith that causes us to hear how to operate and overcome.

The Parrot: Faith Can Invade Your Boundaries

In *Possessing Your Inheritance* I share a story about how I forgot this simple, childlike faith dimension:

> God sees all the war and wilderness places that we have been in. Through those times, He begins to increase our measure of faith. As this childlike faith begins to arise, the glory of God rests down upon us.
>
> I have always considered myself a man of faith. After all, I lead meetings all over the world filled with great faith and expectation of what God will do. Nonetheless, I learned a new lesson about childlike faith recently. In addition to many other responsibilities, I had just begun working with C. Peter Wagner, Doris Wagner and Ted Haggard in a project called the World Prayer Center (WPC). This unique project holds great potential for raising up massive amounts of

prayer throughout the world. It also holds equal potential as a target for spiritual warfare.

My job as executive director of the WPC included leading the intercession needed for raising the necessary funds. Because of the level of warfare we had been in, I knew that I did not have the faith I needed for seeing the project through. One morning I asked the Lord to increase my measure of faith concerning the WPC. That same day I was on my way down to south Texas to lead a revival meeting. As I was preparing to leave, my fifteen-year-old son Daniel came to me and said "Daddy, when you're in south Texas, I believe God wants you to bring me back a parrot."

Chuckling at him I said, "Daniel, parrots cost $1500. Why don't you go ask the Lord if He really wants you to have a parrot. If He does, He'll get one for you." Accepting my statement, Daniel headed out of the room. About ten minuets later, he came back and flatly stated, "Daddy, I asked the Lord about my parrot and He said He wants me to have one." I could not believe it. What could I say? I just left shaking my head and wondering if I had somehow taught him to manipulate what he was hearing from God.

When I got to south Texas I was telling the couple I was staying with about my conversation with Daniel. The man and I just laughed it off. But the wife looked at me and said, "Parrots fly over the border from Mexico through here all the time." I looked at her and wondered what that had to do with anything. We could never catch a wild parrot.

I got up at 5:00 the next morning for my quiet time. In the middle of my devotions, I heard something outside. As I looked out my window, I saw that the woman had set a cage up in a tree and was down on her knees praying. I thought to myself that I had somehow led this woman into total delusion. Did she expect a wild parrot to just walk into the cage? Snickering, I went back and finished my quiet time. Later that morning I led a big prayer meeting, all filled with faith.

The next morning I got up for my quiet time. This time I was in deep prayer for the World Prayer Center—the very thing I needed faith for. Again, I heard something outside. I opened my window and looked outside to see this woman shutting the door of the cage. Inexplicably, a large, beautiful parrot had flown into the yard and walked into the waiting cage all on its own! I looked up at the Lord and said, "Lord I am in bad trouble for my lack of faith." And it just felt like He agreed with me.

That day the Lord began to speak into my heart and say, "Your borders are too narrow. But I can cross your borders, I can bring the supply that's needed. If you will have faith as a child, I will release that which you need in this hour." Today that parrot sits in my house. I can't look at it without being reminded of God's supply in the face of childlike faith. I encourage you that no matter where you are in life, God has a plan to increase your measure of faith![1]

Daniel: Love Is Like a Butterfly Landing

Daniel has taught me a great deal. There was another instance when Daniel was very young that he perceived something that would be harmful. This was a complex future situation that we had to deal with in a simple family setting. In *The Worship Warrior* I share about this account:

> When he was seven years old he came to his mother and me with a question: "What is anthrax?" We both were astonished that a seven-year-old boy would ask such a question. My stepfather (Daniel's grandfather) had cows and land, so I assumed that he had mentioned the issue of anthrax occurring in a natural context. However, when my wife and I questioned Daniel over where he had heard the word "anthrax," he said, "The Lord spoke it to me and said it is coming to America." I explained to him what anthrax was. We have always been honest with our kids, so I just laid it all out on the line. This caused him to fear that it might come upon him. When he would touch something, he would immediately wash his hands. This threw us into a crisis as a family.
>
> In my quiet time one morning I began to seek the Lord, asking Him how He would pull us out of this awkward situation and bring freedom and confidence to Daniel. The Spirit of God said: "This will not be an issue in Daniel's life until he is 20 years old." At breakfast that morning when he began to obsessively discuss anthrax with us, I told him what the Lord had said. Pam gave me that look that said, *Why in the world would you say this so I have to live with his*

obsessive fear for the next 13 years? Nothing really changed, except that I had heard God.

When I do not know what to do, I either worship or ask God what I can give. I find that I can begin to hear Him when I begin to worship, and He will always tell me where to give. Then I can hear Him on the issues that burden my heart. That night when I put Daniel to bed, I said to him, "Let's worship." We listened to a Psalty audiocassette and sang along. At the end of the music, I said to Daniel, "You know how much Mom and I love you. We have tried every way we know to help you get through the fear of what God has shown you. Perfect love casts out all fear. God does not give you the spirit of fear. Therefore, ask the Lord to show you how much He loves you. Since we've worshiped, is there anything you want to ask the Lord?" Daniel replied, "I've been trying to catch a butterfly all week, and I've not been able to."

As any good parent, I wanted to go out and find every butterfly I could find and put them all in his room so that when he awakened, they would be surrounding him. However, I knew I could not do that. I had to trust the Lord. The next morning, when he got up and we were sitting outside, he still feared anthrax. While I was praying for him before I left for work, an interesting thing happened. A butterfly flew into our yard and landed upon Daniel's shirt. He cupped his hands around the butterfly and looked up at the Lord and said, "Because You have shown me how much You love me, I'm just going to set this butterfly free." This was quite a moment.

On Daniel's 20th birthday, the headlines in the newspapers in America read "Anthrax Strikes America." Daniel now works for the law enforcement agency in our region and is enrolled in the police academy. I was traveling and called him on his birthday. Remembering God's word about anthrax, I asked Daniel how he was doing. He said, "Dad, since we worshiped that night and God revealed His love to me the next day, I have never questioned His love over protecting me in the midst of this particular crisis." He had received faith that would last him the next 13 years of his life and extend into the future.

Worship causes us to experience the Father's love. Faith works by love. As we worship, faith is released.[2]

John Mark: Which Communion Is Free?

John Mark is one of our easy-going, fun-loving, yet focused children. He has always been very definitive about what he wants and doesn't want. If he has a question to ask he just simply asks the question. He doesn't seem as complicated emotionally as some of the rest of us. One thing he did as a child really affected me.

I was leading a service at our local church. One of the things that we always did on the first of each month was take communion. We would usually have four tables situated around the sanctuary, and at the end of the service people would bring their offerings and receive the communion elements so that they could participate together and begin their month.

John Mark came up to me in the midst of this service, pulled on my jacket, and said these words: "I don't have any money, so which table is free?"

My eyes were immediately opened to how religiously we think about approaching the Lord. Many of us think that we have to buy our way into Heaven to gain that place of communion where we can hear our Creator speak to us. We don't usually have the confidence to walk, commune, and talk to Him about everything that is going on in our lives. Even the formal religious structures around us have tried to disciple us in the way to touch God and hear Him clearly.

I simply looked down at John Mark and said, "The communion table is free. You do not have to have money to get there. If you will wait, I will just go with you. Matter of fact, we could go to all four tables if we wanted to."

This was a changing point in my own life. The Lord taught me not to let the clutter of the world and all my anxieties linked with money to keep me from coming simply and communing with Him.

Anna: A Child Can Shut the Door to Danger

Brian Kooiman, my assistant, told me a story of his two-year-old daughter, Anna. He said:

One day when my wife, Lori, and I were at the office, Anna drew a picture. Now, to say this was a picture may be a little bit of a stretch. Actually, it was five distinct sets of squiggles that were her best attempt to communicate by writing. When our friend Rose, who helps care for our girls, asked her to explain what she drew, she began by pointing to each one of the squiggles. The first one she explained was "Anna," the next was her younger sister, "Gabi," the third was "Momma," and the fourth was "Papa." The final squiggly line was "danger." Then she said, "Papa...danger."

At this point, she went down the hall to her room and closed her sister's bedroom door and said "safe." Then she closed her bedroom door and said "safe." Then she closed our bedroom door and said "safe." Finally, she closed the hallway bathroom door and said "safe." Having done this, she had completed her intercession and went on to play like nothing happened.

Brian travels extensively with me. Even this small child had shown us that on our path of complexities and dangers throughout our year ahead, she had already prayed and found a way to "shut the door" to the enemy's plans and we would not have to live in anxiety as we go throughout the world.

Ethan: God Can Use a Child to Confirm Your Future

Our lives operate in seasons. We seem to have assignments and press forward in those assignments. Some of our hardest times occur when we end an assignment and are waiting to begin the next phase of our life.

We have to "hear so we know how to follow." Those transitional times can be hard because you are dying to the past season and all of its good and bad. You have a glimpse at times of where you are going, but you are not sure.

Therefore, you are living in confusion. But down deep you know that He has a plan and that you can break into your next new assignment.

This happened to me recently as Dutch Sheets and I finished an assignment that involved going to all 50 states in our nation. This was an 18-month-long assignment. You can read the record of this in *Releasing the Prophetic Destiny of a Nation* (Destiny Image, 2005). When we finished going to the last state, Pennsylvania, I also had another assignment that was coming to completion. I left Pennsylvania to fly to Spain, Italy, and San Marino. I work with Dr. Peter Wagner, a well-known missiologist and church leader, and he had assigned our mission focus as the 40/70 Window. (If you will look on your map, this begins with Iceland, covers all the nations in Europe, moves across northern China and Russian and to the northern tip of Japan.) My responsibility was to get a prayer team into each nation. The tiny republic of San Marino was the last nation for a team to visit. That assignment also was completed.

I noticed on my schedule that there was a week between my international travel and my next speaking engagement. I pulled aside to seek the Lord over what I was to do in the future. The Lord began to give me several key impressions. He began to show me ten months of great change that would come into the earth. He began to tell me how I was to walk during those ten months and communicate to the Body of Christ. What He said created some major changes in my life and the way I was operating in ministry.

I proceeded ahead cautiously but I can't say it was with total confidence. There were such changes ahead that I asked the Lord to confirm that I was on the right path and doing what He asked me to do. I am a man of authority and under authority. I usually seek the older, wiser ones in my life to help me along this path. I was expecting Peter or his wife, Doris, or some of the other leaders in my life to speak to me and confirm exactly what I was doing—little did I know that I would receive confirmation from a completely different and surprising source.

I was beginning to communicate to other people about these ten months of change that were coming in our nation and individual lives. One of my communications even had to do with a warning about what has been recorded as Hurricane Katrina, which hit the Gulf Coast in 2005. The week after the Lord began to impress on me the ten months of changes ahead, I shared that this hurricane was coming. I had entered into a whole new dimension of my gift being used in the Body of Christ. I went to Houston and shared about another hurricane that would come to Galveston. Oh my, was I ever moving in a different dimension! Hurricane Rita later came through that part of our nation. Here I was prophesying all of these major changes to our nation, giving warnings, while needing to come to a different level of confidence in my own life. (By the way, *confidence* is a synonym for *faith*.)

It was January and I went home to spend the weekend with my family. We were planning to watch the Super Bowl together on Sunday. When I got home on Saturday, Pam asked me if Ethan, our youngest, had told me about a dream that he had had the night before, on Friday night. I told her that I had not had a chance to visit with him yet. However, when he walked through our family room, I stopped him and said, "Mom said you had a dream. Would you share it with me?"

He then began to share how in this dream he had seen the final score of the Super Bowl and how the entire game would play out. I was a little surprised. I then told him that sometimes dreams could be from the Lord, and that we would just watch to see how the game finished the next day. Then we would talk about his dream.

The next day the game finished just as he had dreamed! I had a strange feeling come over me. You know the feeling that I am talking about. I don't know whether it's the fear of God or what, but you just have a strange feeling. I asked the Lord, "Why did You give this kid that dream? There are thousands of people all over the world who wanted to have this dream. All of Las Vegas wanted to have this dream!" Not too surprisingly, the Lord did not say anything to me.

That night I went in to pray with Ethan before we went to bed. I reminded him that since his dream was very clear and accurate that perhaps he was a prophet. You know, prophets—those who can see into the future and share things to come or communicate wisdom and counsel for a present situation. I operate in this gift, so I was thinking that perhaps Ethan could be my successor in our family.

The next morning when I was having breakfast with Pam, Ethan came to the table. He said, "Dad, you really think I could be prophetic?"

I said, "Well, you have a pretty good track record with that Super Bowl dream."

He said, "But do you think I am prophetic?"

I simply said, "Yes."

He said, "Well, I had a dream about you last night!"

Oh my, talk about that creepy fear-of-God feeling. He then explained to me that in his dream he had seen me go up a mountain. To get up this mountain, I had to go through TEN DIFFERENT LEVELS. (Now remember that ten-month change in which I am walking.)

He said, "Each one of these levels was like a video game. You had to get past grim reapers (death, confusion, and destruction). Once you got past the ten levels you sat down on top of the mountain and began to sign books like I've seen you do at conferences. You had formed a path for others to follow and they could come and receive your book. I believe, Dad, you have TEN LEVELS TO GET PAST THIS YEAR."

Oh my, out of the mouth of babes! The Lord had used this young man to confirm the path that I was now walking. He had used him to tell me that this path would not be easy and that the things I was communicating would not be easy. However, He also used him to tell me that I would get to my "there." He had even used him to tell me that I would be able to communicate to others how to sidestep the traps that would keep them from pressing through into their future destiny.

Faith has a voice. Many, many times this voice can come through children. The voice is not complex. It is very simple to understand so that we press forward into our path ahead.

Endnotes

1. Chuck D. Pierce and Rebecca Wagner Sytsema, *Possessing Your Inheritance* (Ventura, CA: Renew Books, 1999), 52-54.

2. Chuck D. Pierce with John Dickson, *The Worship Warrior* (Ventura, CA: Regal Books, 2002), 108-110.

Chapter 6

HER NAME
IS MAGGIE:
THE POWER OF ADOPTION

For you did not receive the spirit of bondage again to fear,
but you received the Spirit of adoption
by whom we cry, "Abba, Father."
(Romans 8:15)

W<small>E</small> have talked about children, so now let's shift to animals!

Every June, the City of Denton hosts a special event on the town square called Dog Days of Summer. Vendors of all kinds gather on the courthouse lawn with area humane and animal rescue societies for this unique event. Dog lovers and their beloved pets, prospective dog owners, and people from all over the north Texas area converge on the Courthouse Square in the heat of summer to show their love for and interest in all things canine. (We are dog owners, or should I say, our dogs own us!)

In the summer of 2004, our family decided to drop by the square and see for ourselves just exactly what went on at Dog Days of Summer. We didn't know what to expect because none of us had ever attended the event. After parking several blocks away and walking to the edge of the square, we entered a land of leashed dogs with their owners in tow. Festive canopies sheltered vendors selling homemade dog treats, grooming products, leashes, collars, clothing, and every accessory for the fashion-conscious dog imaginable. Local animal shelter and humane society representatives were positioned strategically around the courthouse to ensure that visitors could see the adorable faces of their caged canines. As we approached the northwest corner of the square, my daughter, Rebekah, and I were irresistibly drawn to the cage of a smiling black and white puppy.

"Oh, my goodness," Rebekah squealed. "She's beautiful!"

"No, absolutely not," I said emphatically. "We already have three dogs."

"That's right," agreed Chuck, "and one of them is neurotic."

"But look, Mom," Rebekah continued shamelessly, "she looks just like Bandit."

Okay, Rebekah was fighting dirty now, bringing up the sweet, old border-collie-mix dog that had grown up with the kids and died five years earlier. I looked closely at the caged puppy. It was true that she was black and white with markings similar to Bandit, but the resemblance stopped there. This dog was lankier than Bandit, with floppy ears and mischievous, amber eyes.

"Oh, for crying out loud," I moaned. I turned to the volunteer from Casa de Critters and asked if we could take the puppy out of the cage.

The puppy's information sheet indicated that she was half Catahoula Leopard dog and half Labrador retriever. She was five months old, had all of her shots, and had just been spayed. When the volunteer brought her out of the cage, the puppy wiggled with enthusiasm and lavished us with affection. Her coat was soft, silky, and slightly wavy. Rebekah and I were smitten at once, but Chuck still was not convinced.

"Let's not jump into this," he cautioned. "Only God in Heaven could convince me to get another dog." After looking at the information sheet more closely, he asked the volunteer, "Why do you call her RCA?"

"We call her that because of her markings and resemblance to the RCA symbol," she replied.

Chuck was trying to divert our attention so the animal shelter volunteers could put the puppy back in her crate and he could get us moving again.

For the next hour, we strolled around the square petting puppies, buying dog treats, and drinking lemonade. Suddenly, Chuck stopped and said, "Her name is Maggie."

"Whose name?" we asked.

He shook his head in resignation and grinned, "That dog. Let's go get her and take her home."

Out of the blue he explained that he had felt a deep impression from the Lord about the black and white dog's name. "Maggie!" So, a fourth dog entered our home. However, if we thought we were ruled before, we were mistaken. This one is the queen of all she sees, including cat, dogs, and humans.

Only the Lord could have told Chuck to get another dog, and He told him quite clearly. In the midst of a crowd on a hot summer day in Denton, Texas, God spoke the name of a dog to my spiritual husband. It didn't matter what name had been assigned to that black and white fur ball; God had already chosen her name, and He knew that Chuck would respond in obedience to His voice.

He Knows Your NAME!

A name is very important. Many of us have never really thought about God knowing our name. In our modern culture, we think our name is just our identifier. Supposedly, names are chosen by our parents because they like the sound of it, or it was popular at the time of our birth. In fact, the census department releases an annual list of the most popular names in our country. Sometimes a name is linked with an ancestor or a person we don't even know. Biblically, however, a name was more than that. Instead, a name represented and defined who the individual was. The name was based upon the character that the individual would display. The name was also linked with the function of the individual.

You may think it strange that the Lord gave me the name for that dog. But I want you to think in terms of yourself. I want you to get past your appearance and think, "What is my function?" Let the Lord redefine you and let Him "name" you. This will be a key to advancing in your future.

He Knows Your Capabilities

Chuck tells this story about our other adopted son, Joseph:

The other supernatural intervention in our lives was Joseph, who came to us at the age of 13 when we were serving as administrators of an institute in Texas for children from dysfunctional homes. (Actually, he came to us as "Billy," nicknamed after one of the men that his natural mother had aligned herself with, but we discovered that his real name was Joseph.) Joseph did not know his natural father, and his mother was in prison. He was a street kid from Houston who had been in numerous foster homes and care group homes. As with many children who come from dysfunctional authority structures in the home, Joseph knew the "system" of how to lie and manipulate to gain favor. However, he did not know the Lord. He had been forced to be religious and to follow rules, but he had no reality of God in his life.

Our role was to lead Joseph to the Lord and fully establish him on the path that God had destined for him when He created him in the womb. We actually knew that we would have to go through a process to redevelop his identity and make him into the "Joseph" that God intended for him to be. He was a trial for us. Not only were we developing his character, but we were also undoing and unraveling many of the ungodly mind-sets of survival that he had developed. Satan had grabbed hold of Joseph's destiny at an early age and was attempting to hold him on a path of destruction.

But God! The promise that God gave me for Joseph was that he would be an "A" and "B" grade student. Oh, my! This was neither a reality nor a desire in his heart. War after war proceeded. He did make enough "C" grades to keep him in sport programs that he enjoyed. But the several severe strongholds caused by the abuses from his past remained and there was constant contention over these issues. Because Joseph knew "the system," our discernment level had to rise so that we could distinguish the truth from the lies in what he told us.

I would love to say that this was an easy war, but that would not be true. I came home one day after a discussion with one of his teachers at school at the end of my rope. I was ready to just let Joseph go down the path that he seemed to desire most. When I walked into the house, Pam turned from the kitchen window and said, "The Lord spoke to me and told me that He was going to fill Joseph with the Holy Spirit." My weariness and unbelief took over and I said, "Oh great, that means I have to endure this war longer." Pam then said, "Well, you can agree with God or agree with what you see!" I chose to submit and trust the word that the Lord had spoken to my wife.

When I did this, two things occurred. First of all, I began to see that Pam had a dimension of faith that I did not have because of her mother's love for a son who had been given to her. Love and faith were working together to bring prophetic fulfillment. Second, I began to see how the enemy used weariness, turmoil, frustration and circumstance to cause me to forget the word of promise and plan of heaven. Remember, the only thing that the Lord had ever spoken to me about Joseph was that he would make A's and B's in school.

I would like to say things turned around immediately, but they did not! After high school, Joseph went to a private college in East Texas and then attended a junior college in North Texas for two years. Yet he was still mediocre at school and still filled with issues. Joseph decided to enter the Air Force, and Pam and I took assignments in New Mexico and Colorado Springs. Joseph married soon after, but his life continued to be up and down. I still wondered in my heart if he would ever really change. But Pam walked in faith and believed in God's promises.

When Joseph was 32, Pam and I moved back to Denton. By this time, Joseph had four children, and he was now attending the University of North Texas and working part-time. When he and his family came for Christmas at our home that year, he shared with me how they had little money because of his working part-time and attending school. However, he did have a special gift for me—it was his final grade report in college. He had gotten all "A's"! He had made the dean's list and finished his schooling, just as the Lord had said in the beginning. He had finished strong! He had proven to the enemy, to himself, and to me that what God had said about him was a reality. Both Joseph and his wife now serve in pastoral ministry. The Lord had fulfilled the word He had spoken to my wife as well. I learned much through watching this orchid bloom![1]

He Knows Where You Should be Positioned

Our name is linked with our authority also. Remember, the Lord said, *"I will do whatever you ask in My name so that the Son may bring glory to the Father"* (John 14:13). Most of us have been taught the Lord's Prayer. If we are Christian and we pray, we pray "in the name of Jesus." This phrase was never meant to be a ritual formalist type of statement. This was meant to connect us with the authority of the One whose name we were using. When we pray in the name of Jesus we are actually praying in His character. We are praying in the same Spirit that He exhibited for us in the earth realm. We are actually identifying with the person to whom we are praying.

This links us with that person's authority where we live in the earth. In other words, we are bringing Heaven down to where we are standing in earth and we are identifying with the name of the One with whom we are connected in Heaven.

So many people are confused about where they should be. Acts 17:24-26 says:

> *God, who made the world and everything in it, since He is Lord of heaven and earth, does not dwell in temples made with hands. Nor is He worshiped with men's hands, as though He needed anything, since He gives to all life, breath, and all things. And He has made from one blood every nation of men to dwell on all the face of the earth, and has determined their preappointed times and the boundaries of their dwellings...."*

Notice these verses say He has predetermined our times and our places. Therefore, if we are confident that He "knows" us, we can be confident that we are walking in His time and His place. We become His ambassador. We know He loves us and wants the best for us on a daily basis. Our identity begins to reflect His identity.

Next time you pray, pray the way that the Lord told us:

Our Father in heaven,
Hallowed be Your name.
Your kingdom come.
Your will be done
On earth as it is in heaven.
Give us this day our daily bread.
And forgive us our debts,
As we forgive our debtors.
And do not lead us into temptation,
But deliver us from the evil one.
For Yours is the kingdom and the power
and the glory forever. Amen
(Matthew 6:9-13).

We Must Learn the Power of Adoption

If He knew Maggie's name, then He certainly knows your name! I want to encourage you that there is One who loves you, who knows everything about you, and wants to adopt you so He can direct your purpose and destiny toward fulfillment. Remember, Chuck and I have actually experienced the power of adoption by adopting two children who are now adults.

We each have to come to the place where we understand this concept of adoption. I think this is one of the biggest problems in society today. So many people feel disconnected, disowned, abandoned. There is a wandering around that is going on in the earth realm today. People don't understand who they are. Therefore, they lose sight of their purpose and function in the earth.

Adoption is a key. Adoption simply means that you receive the privileges of a natural son or daughter. We find examples in the Bible of both male and female experiencing this. Abraham even mentioned that he had adopted his slave, Eliezer, as one of his sons. In Roman culture, the adoption of a stranger into a bloodline caused that stranger to become a member of a family. This tie could not be broken. Usually, the ceremony of adoption took place in front of at least seven witnesses with this statement: "I claim this man (or daughter or slave) as my son (or daughter or slave)." That is why in the New Testament adoption was used as an important concept of our relationship with the Lord. Therefore, we are fully reinstated from a lost state of privileges into all the privileges of God the Father.

Adoption is a positional word, not just a relational word. I think many people do not understand their time or place since they don't understand the position of adoption they have with their Creator or Father.

Many people never really experience God's love for them. Maggie, our dog, now knows that we love her. She even knows her position in our house. Let me remind you of a verse in the Book of Matthew: *"Look at the birds of the air, for they neither sow nor reap nor gather into barns; yet your heavenly Father feeds them. Are you not of more value than they?"* (Matt. 6:26).

He knows your name.

Endnote

1. Chuck D. Pierce and Rebecca Wagner Sytsema, *God's Now Time For Your Life* (Ventura, CA: Regal Books, 2005), 126-129.

Chapter 7

PLEASE PASS THE BISCUITS:
FINDING YOUR WAY THROUGH DISCIPLINE

Do you ever look back over your past and feel as though you have lived several different lives? I do. Because of all the changes and transitions through which the Lord has brought me, I can see my life in segments that seem so different from each other that I wonder how they could all fit together. This doesn't mean that I suffer from multiple personality disorder; it simply means that God, in His mercy, has never given up on His plan to change me into the image of His Son. And I can say, with some degree of confidence, that when I am 80 years old I will still be changing.

The first segment of life that I actually remember was my early childhood years in Southern California. When I was a toddler, my family moved from East Texas—where my dad was an engineer for a gas company—and settled in La Puente. Since I was still too young to be aware of my parents as individuals with a life apart from my own needs, it was a carefree, sunny time of outdoor play, scrapes, bruises, broken bones, and dogs.

By the time we moved to Huntsville, Alabama, I had started to notice that my parents had some problems—problems related to alcohol. My older sister, Paula, felt these problems more acutely than I did. I was still young and self-centered enough to indulge my need for fun as often as possible. That brief sojourn in Alabama was like an adventure for me: following the creek in search of tadpoles, catching jars full of fireflies, taking trips to the emergency room for stitches, and hiding from my grandmother in the big, blue hydrangea bushes. It was also the period when my natural inclination for mischief rose to the surface like lava from a volcano. I was mischievous to the point of being dangerous!

We returned to California several months later and settled in West Covina. Paula and I knew that our parents were in serious trouble, but pouring their liquor down the kitchen drain didn't seem to help much. On Christmas Eve, when I was in the third grade, our parents had a serious car accident on the way home from shopping. This was before people wore seat belts in their cars, so my mother was thrown through the windshield and sustained extensive injuries to her face. The next thing I knew, Paula and I were flying out to Arkansas to stay with our Aunt Nancy and Uncle Kenneth.

After several months, Paula and I returned home to a mother we hardly recognized. As her facial scars continued to heal, everything else fell apart. Over the next several months, both of my parents became more dependent on alcohol and less available as parents. We moved several times. I went to four different elementary schools that year. Finally, my dad decided that we needed to pack up the car and go live with his parents in Lake Jackson, Texas, until we could get through this difficult time.

Living with my grandparents was actually a joy. Although they both looked ancient to me, they were full of life. My grandmother taught us how to make clothes for our Barbie dolls, and my grandfather let me help in the kitchen. Both of them told us stories about their early years in Missouri, and Paula and I would beg to hear more. There were always neighborhood kids to play with, woods and creeks to explore, and the beach was just a short drive from the house.

After our brief stay in Lake Jackson, my dad took a job with a chemical company in Houston. We moved into a furnished apartment just two blocks from the Shamrock Hilton Hotel. I started the fifth grade in the fall of 1963. Because of my erratic life over the past few years, I was a less-than-ideal student. The only thing I was really good at was spelling, writing, and getting into trouble. My best friend Vicki, her sister Terri, Paula, and I rode the city buses that year and shared adventures all over Houston. At the same time, my parents spiraled further and further out of control. The more they drank, the more Paula and I stayed away. We found refuge at our friends' houses, on the city buses, at the park, museums, and movie theaters.

When the school year ended, we moved again—this time to another job and another furnished apartment in Bay City. Less than a week after we moved, however, my dad came home one night without the car. Paula and I walked all over town looking for the car while our parents slept. I'll never forget how the heat rose from the pavement in waves. I'll also never forget how many dead armadillos littered the streets on that hot summer day!

It wasn't long after this fruitless quest for the missing car that one of our aunts from Lake Jackson arrived. She packed Paula's and my clothes, loaded us into her car, and drove several hours to our maternal grandmother's house in East Texas. Within a week, our grandmother had bought Paula and me some new clothes and shoes and drove us to the airport in Shreveport, Louisiana. She had already told us that we were going to live with our Aunt Betty and Uncle Clint in New England. Considering the fact that I had failed social studies in the fourth grade, I thought that meant we were going to England, home of the Beatles!

Paula was very solemn during the long plane ride to Boston and hardly said a word. I didn't know why she wasn't excited about a new adventure, but I was determined to have a good time. We had only met our mother's sister, Betty, a few times over the years, but we had always enjoyed playing with our two cousins, Mark and Mike. As for our Uncle Clint, well, he was a bit of an unknown factor, but I was sure he'd be okay.

Boston's Logan Airport was dark, cold, and rainy when we arrived. The stewardess (not "flight attendant"—remember, it was the 1960s) helped us deplane and find our new family before waving good-bye. Suddenly, I realized that this whole thing was real and I was a long way from everything familiar. I looked at my aunt, uncle, and two cousins and said, "Hi! We like the Beatles." Brilliant.

I had spent the first 11 years of my life moving, adapting, and fighting for my place of security. I knew from the first day in this new place that it was going to be different.

Paula and I slept in an upstairs bedroom in a 200-year-old farmhouse that night. The rain was still falling as we fell into exhausted sleep. The next morning, I awoke to the sound of fluttering curtains and softly clucking chickens. As I opened my eyes, I saw a rectangle of bright blue sky through the open window. The air smelled of lilac and freshly mown grass. I slipped out from under the covers and squatted in front of the south-facing window. A three-story red barn dominated the landscape to the left of the window.

Beyond that stretched a forest of pointed firs, birches, and maples. The backdrop for all of this beauty was a soft green mountain with a bald spot on top. A blue-gray mist crouched near the base of the mountain. Even as I watched, the sun warmed a little and the mist started to dissipate.

I didn't know it then, but my aunt and uncle had been trying to convince my parents to let Paula and I come live with them for quite awhile. They understood the severity of my parents' problems. Obviously, my parents finally admitted to themselves and their families that Paula and I needed more stability in our lives. Surely an Air Force Chief Master Sergeant and his schoolteacher wife could provide that stability!

From the beginning, I had a hard time accepting boundaries and discipline from these "stand-in" parents. I had been doing just fine on my own, thank you very much, and I didn't need strangers telling me what to do. I was used to eating when I wanted, what I wanted, and where I wanted. All of a sudden, I had to show up at the kitchen table three times a day. Not only that, I actually had to set the table and help wash the dishes after meals! As if that weren't enough, I was expected to do "chores" around the house, bathe regularly, and brush my teeth, for goodness' sake!

As you can imagine, my stubborn, mischievous streak was stirred up heartily. It quickly became apparent that, although Paula was fitting in quite nicely, I was not. I resented everything: sharing a bathroom with two cousins, having an actual bedtime, going to church. You name it, I resented and rebelled against it. I became so belligerent that my aunt finally told my uncle that she couldn't do anything with me.

"She is going to have to go to a foster home," she told my uncle when he returned home from the Air Force base one night. "Paula can stay, but Pamela has to go."

It was obvious that my uncle had put a lot of thought into his reply.

"No," he said, "I have a better idea. Just let me work with Pam. You don't even worry about what she does—just turn her over to me."

My aunt's relief was apparent. (Years later, my uncle told us that the reason we didn't get along during those early years was because we were so much alike.) She agreed to the new arrangement and symbolically turned me over to my Air Force uncle. Oh, boy!

Sometimes basic training is just what we need to change old patterns of behavior and thinking. That conversation marked the beginning of a whole new life for me. I didn't know it yet, but the Lord was about to bring order out of chaos through my uncle.

Like the centurion soldier in Matthew 7, Clint Hughes understood authority because he was a man under authority. When his commanding officer gave him an order, he didn't grumble or try to argue his way out of that order. His Air Force training had prepared him to oversee critical tasks on the flight line during the Vietnam War. When he told an airman to do something, he expected that airman to obey without argument. He had also been raised during an era when hard work was expected and respected, and he recognized the value of discipline and commitment to a job.

The first thing my uncle did was to establish a consistent routine for me and teach me how to contribute to the household in a tangible way. He tutored me on the feeding and care of chickens, including the sometimes risky business of gathering eggs out from under a hen! He taught me how to start a fire in our basement's wood-burning stove on cold, New Hampshire mornings before anyone else was awake.

He put me to work in the vegetable garden, weeding and harvesting. And he showed me how to make biscuits.

The first time Uncle Clint turned me loose with flour and shortening, I baked a lovely batch of hockey pucks. Honestly, I don't know how he managed to keep showing me the fine art of biscuit making without pulling out my hair (his was already too thin to pull).

"You're kneading them too much," he kept saying.

"That doesn't make any sense," I insisted. "How can that make so much difference?"

"Trust me, Miss Unteachable. It does. Now try again."

And I would try again and again. Then, finally, I made the most beautiful batch of fluffy, golden-brown biscuits you've ever seen. We almost held our breaths as Uncle Clint pierced the side of one fragrant biscuit with a fork. The fork slid into the soft, round pillow with no resistance and released a little cloud of steam. I had done it!

Responsibility, hard work, and a job well done were just what I needed. When everyone else saw a stubborn, rebellious redhead, my uncle saw someone who needed to be valued as a contributing member of a family. No one had ever taken the time to help me discover that I could actually make something besides trouble. Even though I still had plenty of behavioral and spiritual problems, my uncle had put me on the road to recovery and to the Lord. And it all started with biscuits.

Proverbs 22:6 says, *"Train up a child in the way he should go, and when he is old he will not depart from it."* My natural parents had abdicated their God-given responsibility to train me in any way. I had been allowed to rule myself most of my young life, and I had done a lousy job! My unrestricted freedom had produced someone with no self-control, no discipline, no respect for others, and no sense of purpose. My retraining would require self-control, discipline, and respect for others, but for the first time in my life I had a sense of purpose.

My uncle gave me a precious gift when he enrolled me in his home version of basic training. He spent time with me and imparted his knowledge and expertise. But even more than that, he loved me. Even when he was grounding me—again—I knew he loved me. His training was consistent and included a healthy dose of humor. It also included frequent camping weekends to the White Mountains and trips to the Maine coast for fresh seafood!

As I have raised my own children, I have attempted to find the "biscuit" in each of their lives. In other words, I recognize, as a person and as a parent, how important it is to do (at least) one thing well. For one it might be a unique artistic ability; for another, it might be a gift for writing; for another it might be a musical gift, and for another, an aptitude for athletics. All of these things pale, however, compared to knowing God well.

Until I went to live with my aunt and uncle in New Hampshire, I had only been to church a few times. My maternal grandmother always took me to church with her when we went to visit in East Texas. I remembered going to church once when we lived in California and a few times when we lived in Lake Jackson. On Easter Sunday in 1964, my parents, Paula, and I got all dressed up for church. We left the apartment in Houston searching for a church and finally stopped at a movie theater. Our Easter service that day consisted of eating popcorn and watching *Mary Poppins*.

That changed drastically when Paula and I moved in with our aunt and uncle. They loved the Lord with all their hearts and were active in their little church across the river in Maine. The new discipline of church attendance introduced me to a whole new world. I fell in love with Jesus little by little until I finally came face-to-face with the chaos of my own soul in 1971. It's been quite a trip since then!

In 1965, after the death of our natural father, Aunt Betty and Uncle Clint adopted Paula and me. We had been living with them for about nine months, and I had not made the transition easy on anyone. Even so, my aunt and uncle took the plunge and made it official: they now had two daughters. With the adoption came the legal name change, and with that came the opportunity to embrace a new identity.

I have been doubly blessed with two adoptions: natural and spiritual. When my new parents committed themselves to me through the act of adoption, they demonstrated unconditional love and compassion to an unlovable 12-year-old. They knew that my road to emotional and spiritual health would be difficult, but they were willing to walk me down that road. My two cousins, who became my brothers, made the same commitment. I'm sure they questioned the wisdom of that move when I took my problems out on them over and over again!

My natural adoption made my subsequent spiritual adoption easier to embrace and comprehend. Because someone had already loved me enough to adopt me in the flesh, I could identify more readily with the concept of spiritual adoption. I could also acknowledge to myself and others that my spiritual adoption didn't hinge on my perfection, but on faith.

In Romans 8:15 we read, *"For you did not receive the spirit of bondage again to fear, but you received the Spirit of adoption by whom we cry out, 'Abba, Father.'"* When I was adopted, both naturally and spiritually, the bondage of my past began to crumble. The fear of abandonment that plagued me had to release its grip when the Spirit of adoption took its rightful place of authority in my life. In spite of our differences and conflicts over the years, I knew that my new, natural father wouldn't abandon or disown me. Because of his example, it was easier for me to believe that my Heavenly Father would not abandon or disown me either, no matter how many times I failed to meet His high standards. My adopted parents committed to my restoration while my Heavenly Father committed to my rebirth.

My dad went home to be with the Lord last year. He left behind an adoring wife, 4 children, and 12 grandchildren. When the honor guard at his military burial knelt in front of my mother and handed her the folded flag, it was presented from "a grateful nation." The nation's gratitude can't begin to compare with my own.

Chapter 8

THE CAT IN THE CUPBOARD:

FINDING YOUR PLACE OF SECURITY IN THE MIDST OF CHANGE

Peace I leave with you, My peace I give to you;
not as the world gives do I give to you.
Let not your heart be troubled...."
(John 14:27)

O<small>UR</small> youngest son, Ethan, has a cat. She is a black and gray tabby with greenish-gold eyes and a superior attitude. When this cat moved into the house in 2001, she was six weeks old, adorable, and scared of everything. During the first week, the kitten disappeared for several hours. When she finally woke up and came out from under the entertainment center, we named her Cheshire Cat in honor of the vanishing feline in *Alice in Wonderland*. We call her Chessie.

Chessie seemed to fit in with Casey, our big, lovable Golden Retriever mix and Dutch, our cranky brown Dachshund. In fact, Dutch and Casey actually liked Chessie once they got to know her, and the three animals settled into domestic bliss with no trouble at all. The cat slept and ate in Ethan's room, went in and out of the house through the pet door, and grew comfortable with her environment. Like most cats I have known, Chessie kept to herself unless she needed something and watched us humans like we were an elaborate science experiment.

Then Rebekah brought home Wilber. Wilber is a Rottweiler/Australian Shepherd mix who looks more like a black lab with a white patch on his chest. As a puppy, Wilber was cute, floppy, and cuddly. He was also a real challenge to house train because Rebekah's gift of mercy got in the way of crate training. Nevertheless, after replacing most of the carpet in the house with hard floors, Wilber finally got the message about going outside to relieve himself.

The addition of another dog to the house was disconcerting to Chessie. Until Wilber grew beyond the cat's power of control, the two animals avoided each other whenever possible. However, as soon as Wilber realized that he was bigger than Chessie, all bets were off. Poor Chessie couldn't leave Ethan's room for fear that Wilber would chase her through the house. We finally took the screen off Ethan's bedroom window so the cat could use that as her entrance and exit.

For a while, Chessie enjoyed a peaceful existence under Ethan's protection. Then we went to Dog Days of Summer on the town square and came home with Maggie. (You've probably realized by now that we have problem with collecting dogs.) She took one look at Chessie and decided she was a wonderful new toy. Together, Maggie, who is now "Queen of Everything," and Wilber initiated Chessie's involuntary exercise program and chased her into the backyard at every opportunity. Chessie could find her way back to Ethan's room when the coast was clear or Maggie and Wilbur were sleeping.

During this time period, Casey went to live with our son John in his new home, poor old Dutch died of congestive heart failure, and Rebekah started volunteering at the McKinney, Texas, SPCA. When we went to visit the animal shelter with her one afternoon, we came home with—you guessed it—another dog. This time, it was an Australian Cattle Dog-Terrier mix named Charlie. Ethan set up a crate in his room and faithfully house trained the puppy through the difficult first months. As for Chessie, she decided that the master bedroom was a much better place to sleep, even though Chuck is not a cat lover. Fortunately for the cat, Chuck enjoys accumulating frequent flyer miles.

Chessie found her new place of peace in the armoire. There, on top of Chuck's T-shirts, the cat felt secure and out-of-reach of the dogs. Chuck has a strong sense of justice and recognized Chessie's dilemma, so he allowed her to use that space for a refuge. But when Charlie finished crate training and started sleeping in the master bedroom as well, Chessie once again felt pushed out of her place. The next night, when I went to the kitchen for a drink, there she was: in the kitchen cupboard, peacefully sleeping with the water glasses.

Of all the cats we have ever owned, Chessie has proven to be the most resilient and adaptable. Not long after the cupboard incident, Chessie decided on her new course of action. She made it clear to us that she was no longer comfortable indoors and wanted to be fed outside. Her current routine involves spending the night in our converted garage where she can come and go through the pet door with no interference from the dogs. Every morning, we put fresh food and water on the front porch so that Chessie can peacefully eat where the dogs are not allowed to go. Charlie, who turned out to be a small dog, is the only canine Chessie will tolerate. The dog and cat, similar in size and color, chase each other around the front yard while I garden. And no matter how hard we try, Chessie will not come back into the main part of the house with Maggie and neurotic Wilber.

This proves that any of us can adapt to our changing environment and actually find our enlarged place of fulfillment.

Breaking the Hold of Insecurity

Insecurity overtakes so many of us in the midst of changing times. Most of us are not as resilient as Chessie. We are constantly trying to hang on to the comfortable place we had before change invaded our boundaries.

Change can come in so many different ways. The birth of a child can produce change. A new relationship can produce change. Innovation can produce change. Death can produce change. Expanding job duties can produce change. Maturing children can bring change to the whole environment in which we live. Positional changes, including geographical relocation, can really produce insecurities within us.

I believe the key to security is learning to embrace change. Insecurity is actually linked with these five major issues:

1. **The first is FEAR.** We have a measure of fear until we understand how to process what has

invaded our territory. This comes from the unknown aspect of not understanding fully what has come into our scope.

2. **The second factor is CONTROL.** We lose control of a space in which we had developed a routine. We feel like our hands are being pried away from what we were comfortable manipulating.

3. **The third is IGNORANCE or lack of understanding.** A people perish because of "lack of knowledge." The Bible also says a people perish because they do not have vision or prophetic revelation (see Prov. 29:18). Additionally, the Bible says superstition is a sign of ignorance. Ignorance is not simply having a lack of knowledge. Rather, ignorance occurs when we do not embrace the truth that accompanies the changes in our present situation. Ignorance can also occur when we are not willing to expand our horizon and develop new skills to meet our changing environment. Not knowing that there is other truth or revelation linked with the matter that we are dealing with can also lead us into ignorance.

4. **The fourth is SELFISHNESS.** We like our space the way we like it. We don't want to give up anything for the new invader or change catalyst.

5. **The fifth is PRIDE.** Insecurity is just pride masked. We are afraid to fail when we have to expand the place of our tent. We could conclude that pride is fear of failure, ignorance, selfishness, and control all mixed together. We exalt our knowledge above that to which we need to submit rather than embracing our

changing circumstances. Pride is the enemy of our Creator. Pride says, "The one who knows the best for you or the one who has brought change into your life is holding out on you or creating chaos in your life." Don't listen to this voice in your changing circumstances.

Be like Chessie—adapt to that which has created upheaval around you. She could not be happier. She has found her newly enlarged place and enjoys a freedom that the dogs will never attain. She seems to rule all the dogs now. When they go outside, she is the monarch of the expanded domain. She lies atop the garden chest on our front porch and slaps at the dogs as they pass by on their leashes.

Find Your Place of Security in the Future

One of the best examples of being secure and securing your future is from the Book of Ruth, chapter 3:1, which says, *"Then Naomi said to Ruth, 'My daughter, shall I not seek SECURITY (or rest) or a home for you, that you may prosper?'"* Ruth is one of my (Chuck's) favorite stories in the Bible. Our lives have been restored in the midst of major changes, both good and bad. Rebecca Wagner Sytsema and I co-authored a book called *Possessing Your Inheritance*. This book is still one of my favorites, and has a wonderful section on Ruth. The following excerpt is from that book:

The story opens with Naomi, whose family had great wealth and inheritance, living in Bethlehem. But famine began to overtake the city of Bethlehem.

Not knowing what to do the whole family left that area, left their inheritance behind and went to Moab. Naomi's two sons married in the new land and later died there. Naomi's husband also died there. Famine, death, and desolation caused all hope for inheritance to be lost. Naomi had absolutely nothing left but two daughters-in-law, one of whom was Ruth.

Naomi, whose name meant pleasant, had nothing in her heart but bitterness. She even declared that she was to be called "bitter." The enemy can so assault us in our lives that the very opposite of what God intends for us becomes our identity. For Naomi that meant that her pleasantness had turned to bitterness. Yet, she remembered that the inheritance her family once had was back in Bethlehem, not in Moab, so she decided to go back.

Naomi brought her two daughters-in-law together and told them that she could not promise them a better life in Bethlehem because when she left, it was in desolation. One daughter-in-law decided to stay in Moab. God has places of choice for us. When we get to a key deciding place in our life, we find a biblical principle at work: God always gives us the opportunity to go all the way or to turn around and go back.[1]

This is a very important statement in the process of change. We will go forward and embrace those circumstances that create a different environment around us. Ruth served Naomi faithfully by gleaning in the harvest fields around her. However, there comes a time when you must choose to change or your present state of "gleaning" will become the pattern and boundary for your future. Ruth and

Naomi couldn't keep going this way. This gleaning wasn't getting them anywhere. There came a time when Naomi decided to seek security for Ruth. She wanted to secure the best the Lord had for Ruth's future.

Ruth's story continues in *Possessing Your Inheritance*:

> She (Naomi) realized that Boaz was a relative and there was a spiritual law over the area that provided for a relative to bring them back into their inheritance. Suddenly a light went on in her mind. God established provision for them in the Levitical law that said they had a right to family inheritance if the relative would become their kinsman redeemer.

So, Naomi laid out a plan for Ruth to secure her inheritance. This is what she told her to do:

1. **Wash yourself.** Ruth had been gleaning in the fields. She was tired and smelled. Naomi knew they were not going to come into any inheritance with the way Ruth looked. So Ruth brought the water and began to wash herself. Today the Lord is sweeping across His body with cleansing revelation. We have worked hard. We have toiled in the fields and God says "Stop. Wash yourself. Let the word of God flow over you. Take a rest. Soak for a little while and allow the cleansing to refresh and renew."

2. **Anoint yourself.** To anoint means to be smeared with fragrant oil. Ruth needed a new fragrance for the new season. Isaiah 61 speaks of the oil of joy that replaces the mourning in our souls. This

is also a part of Jubilee. Ruth had not been in a season of joy. Rather, she had been in widowhood. But in order to move into her season of inheritance, she needed a new anointing of oil that would emit a pleasant fragrance. As you move into your season of inheritance, allow the Holy Spirit to cover you with a new anointing. Allow the oil of joy to replace the unpleasant odor of mourning in your life.

3. **Put on your best garment.** The garment that Ruth had been wearing to work in the field was inappropriate. Remember Ruth was still in her widow's garment. In order to secure her future the widowhood that was dressed up around her had to come off. The grief that she had been wearing was no good for the next place. It would not draw anyone to her. Like Joseph, Ruth needed to put on a new garment to move into her next place. Here is a lesson for us: Take off the grief. We go through hard, hard things as people. But when God says it's time to change your garments and remove your grief, don't let any self-pity keep that old garment buttoned up on you. Can we draw in the people of the world if we are clothed with grief? No. God is going to have us put on a new garment that will show the world the comfort and encouragement they need. Just as Ruth and Joseph did, get ready to take off that old garment and put on a whole new mantle.

4. **Go to the threshing floor.** The threshing floor had a dual purpose in those days. First, it was where the wheat and the chaff were separated. But it was also a place of feasting. So here Naomi

says, "Ruth I want you to go down to where the party is going on." As we make ourselves ready, God is preparing a feast for us and He is preparing us to go where the party is happening.

5. **Wait for God's timing.** Naomi told Ruth not to enter into the party right away. She was to stand back and wait until all the fun stopped and then come out of the shadows. God is getting us established in our abiding place so we are ready when the time comes. Then Ruth was to go lay down at Boaz's feet and as she did, there would be a distinct decision made. Can you imagine what must have been going on in Ruth's mind? She was a virtuous woman. And now she was told to lay down at the feet of a man. This was a true test of submission. God is bringing the body of Christ to His feet and we are to stay there until we receive the best...Boaz woke from his sleep and saw Ruth lying there. Then Boaz, a beautiful picture of our kinsman redeemer in the Lord Jesus, asked her who she was. Ruth identified herself as a close relative and asked him to draw her in and cover her. Fuchsia Pickett describes Ruth's request this way, "In asking for Boaz to cover her, Ruth was declaring, 'I need a redeemer. I am a widow, disgraced, with no inheritance. You can take my shame, my poverty, the bleakness of my future and give a new beginning."[2]

Ruth was willing to make big changes to secure her future and that of her mother-in-law. As you already know, Boaz married her and everyone received the best of the redeemed time. That is what happens when we are willing to embrace change and find our new place.

When you allow change to produce your new enlarged place, you find that you have increased your security level.

Actually, the Bible defines this as our abiding place. Psalm 91 says:

> *He who dwells in the secret place of the Most High shall abide under the shadow of the Almighty. I will say of the Lord, "He is my refuge and my fortress; my God, in Him I will trust." Surely He shall deliver you from the snare of the fowler and from the perilous pestilence. He shall cover you with His feathers, and under His wings you shall take refuge; His truth shall be your shield and buckler. You shall not be afraid of the terror by night, nor of the arrow that flies by day, nor of the pestilence that walks in darkness, nor of the destruction that lays waste at noonday. A thousand may fall at your side, and ten thousand at your right hand; but it shall not come near you. Only with your eyes shall you look, and see the reward of the wicked. Because you have made the Lord, who is my refuge, even the Most High, your dwelling place, no evil shall befall you, nor shall any plague come near your dwelling; for He shall give His angels charge over you, to keep you in all your ways. In their hands they shall bear you up, lest you dash your foot against a stone. You shall tread upon the lion and the cobra, the young lion and the serpent you shall trample underfoot. "Because he has set his love upon Me, therefore I will deliver him; I will set him on high, because he has known My name. He shall call upon Me, and I will*

answer him; I will be with him in trouble; I will deliver him and honor him. With long life I will satisfy him, and show him My salvation."

This speaks of the great protection we can enjoy by being in the right place at the right time. In the midst of bioterrorism warnings, flu epidemics, and terrorist threats, this Psalm brings me great solace.

Securing Your Portion

"I will fasten him as a peg in a secure place" (Isa. 22:23).

Possessing Your Inheritance continues as follows:

To secure means to put beyond the hazard of losing. It means to bring something to a place of hope or safety; to be fastened, planted and established. When we secure something, we have removed it from exposure to danger. Secure also means to have a feeling of trust or confidence. When we don't have confidence it means we have lost a place of security within us. But God longs to fasten us in a secure place.

As Matthew 6:19 reminds us, our security does not come from treasures stored up for ourselves here on earth where moth and rust destroy and thieves break in and steal—or where the stock market can crash. Our security must be firmly fastened in God.

When we have that in order, then we can secure our inheritance. That does not mean we will never experience any loss.... But it does mean that anything we have has been given to us by God, and as long as we position ourselves correctly in the Lord, the inheritance God has for us is securely fastened in Him.[3]

Security in the Time of Trouble

Where we live and why we live there are both part of our abiding or security. As a child, Pam moved from place to place. Eventually, her family fell apart and she was adopted into a military family that moved from place to place. She had to become secure. We can separate our spiritual abiding place from our physical abiding place, but touching God in the midst of the physical habitat is key to our lives being free from anxiety. Acts 17:26 says that He predetermines the place that you're to seek Him. In that predetermined physical place, you will begin to find Him spiritually and gain the strategy necessary to secure your portion.

Here are some keys to secure your place:

1. THINK differently! Let new ways of thinking about yourself and those that you are aligned with develop.

2. Make any changes necessary in developing skills that will help you advance.

3. Receive MERCY and GRACE to get beyond any failures or faults from your past that hold you captive and make you feel condemned.

4. FORGIVE and release anyone so you are fully released to advance into the best ahead. Forgiveness breaks all the schemes of the enemy.

5. BREAK the power that pulls you back into an old, comfortable place or form of worship. Find creative ways to prosper in your new place instead of longing for the securities of your past.

6. Do not let fear and unbelief keep you from entering into WAR for the fulfillment of your destiny.

7. RECEIVE THE BANNER FOR YOUR FUTURE. His Banner over you is Love. Let Jehovah Nissi arise in your midst.

Come into your new place and let all mistrust and wounds from the past remain in the old place you vacated.

Just remember Chessie: she is breathing the outside air and sees more of us coming and going than she did before she shifted. She rules the whole yard now, not just one room inside the house.

Endnotes

1. Chuck D. Pierce and Rebecca Wagner Sytsema, *Possessing Your Inheritance* (Ventura, CA: Regal Books, 1999), 211-212.

2. Ibid., 212-214.

3. Ibid., 200.

Chapter 9

RESPITE FROM THE STORMS:
FINDING PLACES OF REFUGE FROM THE CHAOS

THERE is no denying it: This world is a chaotic place, full of confusion, heartache, and evil. And yet, we know that God provides places of refuge for His people, sometimes in the midst of terrible circumstances. We have already considered Elijah's precarious position after defeating the priests of Baal. He was running from Jezebel, hiding in the wilderness, when God called him up to the mountain. There on the mountain Elijah found a little cave to huddle into while the wind, earthquake, and fire passed. Then, when the prophet heard the still, small voice of God, *"he wrapped his face in his mantle and went out and stood in the entrance of the cave"* (1 Kings 19:13).

I don't know about you, but I really appreciate those little caves that God provides along the way. These little pockets of refuge provide more than just shelter from the storms of life; they can also be sources of restoration and clarity that we all need from time to time. Whether the chaos of the moment comes from trauma, stress, overwork, loss, or the everyday details of life, there are places we can go for relief. I'm not just referring to spiritual places of safety and restoration, but physical, mental, and emotional ones as well.

We know from the Gospel accounts that even Jesus, the Son of God incarnate, had places of refuge during His time on earth. Jesus regularly separated Himself from His disciples and the eager crowds of people to spend time alone with His Father in prayer and fellowship. Can you imagine being an invisible observer at one of those sessions? On other occasions, Jesus found rest and comfort in the Bethany home of Lazarus, Mary, and Martha. He could even set aside His busy ministry of healing and deliverance to spend time with His disciples, share meals with His friends, and take a stroll through a grain field on the Sabbath.

In Matthew 11:28, Jesus says, *"Come to Me, all you who labor and are heavy laden, and I will give you rest."* More than anyone else, Jesus can identify with our need to pull aside from the cares of the world and regroup before going out to face another chaotic day. *"For He knows our frame,"* says Psalm 103, *"He remembers that we are dust."* He knows that we are body, soul, and spirit, and all three parts require refreshment.

This refreshment may not always come in the way we expect. Have you ever noticed that what is restorative and enjoyable for one person borders on torture for another? I had a friend in Houston who couldn't wait to get home from work every afternoon so she could lace on her Nikes and go for a five-mile run. During that time, she would clear her head of the day's confusion and reconnect with the Lord. Her afternoon run was so important to her well-being that she would run in any kind of weather. When the afternoon heat became intolerable, she would drive several miles to an indoor track and run.

I never understood her need to run. Anything over a five-minute jog was more than I could tolerate. Walking was—and still is—enjoyable for me, but all that running around in circles never appealed to me at all. For my friend in Houston, running provided just what she needed to feel fresh, clear, and restored—even though she would be dripping with sweat by the time she returned home. Personally, I would rather spend that same amount of time working up a sweat in my garden.

And the Earth Brought Forth Grass

I had never given much thought to plants until I worked for the Extension Horticulture department at Texas A&M University. All day, five days a week, I was surrounded by people who were passionate about fruits, nuts, vegetables, and ornamental plants. Those horticulturists were obsessed with developing disease resistant crape myrtles, perfecting the hydroponic tomato, exploring the hidden value of the onion, and educating Texans about the latest landscape gardening innovations. It wasn't long before I was collecting coins from the sofa so that I could buy cuttings from a local nursery. By the time Chuck and I left Texas A&M, our balcony looked like a jungle! That was the beginning of my love for gardening.

Genesis 2:8 says, "*The Lord God planted a garden eastward in Eden, and there He put the man whom He had formed.*" God planted a garden and put Man in it. What a concept! (Adam's son, Cain, was also a gardener; he could have given gardeners a bad name, but there have been plenty of gardeners down through the centuries who didn't murder their rancher brothers in a fit of jealousy and rage.) When I am down on my muddy knees digging in the earth, I feel restored and reconnected to the Lord just like my running friend in Houston.

I realize that not everyone shares my passion for digging, planting, weeding, and growing things, and that's okay. Gardening is one of those little caves God has provided for me in the midst of the world's chaos. No matter how confusing life becomes, I can feel the tension and anxiety drain away through my hands in the warm soil. Like Adam and Eve, I can hear the *"sound of the Lord God walking in the garden in the cool of the day"* (Gen. 3:8), but I don't have to hide myself from His presence. On the contrary, the garden is one place I can consistently go to experience His presence when no one else is around to distract me.

There are as many places of refuge from the chaos as there are individuals in God's Kingdom. God is creative enough to provide each of us with unique places and methods for refreshing. Gardening may not be your choice, and it's certainly not my only one. That's a good thing, since it would leave me without options in the middle of the winter!

Exploring Strange, New Worlds

Gardening is a physical and mental activity that restores me on an emotional and spiritual level. One of my other caves of refuge is totally different and requires no physical exertion: my regular appointments with science fiction.

Let me explain. I have enjoyed reading and watching science fiction since I was a child. Even back in the sixties, when the television production values of science fiction were unbelievably cheesy, I faithfully watched *Lost in Space*, *Star Trek*, and *The Twilight Zone*. Whenever a new science fiction program launched, I tuned in and immersed myself in all the fantastic possibilities the genre affords. Throughout junior high and high school, I combed the library for books by Bradbury, Asimov, Verne, and Wells. Before I even knew about the places of refuge God could provide, I was escaping the chaos of my childhood through the imagination.

After my salvation in 1971, I discovered that the Word of God had so much more to offer than the "strange new worlds" sought by Captain Kirk on the *Enterprise*. I had been reading the Bible for several years, but once I saw it through spiritual eyes it was a whole new book. I was captivated by the characters, the stories, the concepts, and even the villains. One thing that continues to intrigue me about the Bible is the idea of what God *doesn't* tell us. I mean, think about it: there is no way that God put every detail about every thing in that one volume. There are unlimited heavenly libraries full of amazing information awaiting us. My life-long enjoyment of science fiction has developed my imagination in ways that continually enhance my appreciation of God's wonders.

In his book *Oswald Chambers: The Best From All His Books*, Oswald Chamber's has this to say about the imagination: "There is a domain of our nature which we as Christians do not cultivate much, viz., the domain of the imagination. Almost the only way we use our imagination is in crossing bridges before we come to them. The religion of Jesus embraces every part of our make-up, the intellectual part, the emotional part, no part must be allowed to atrophy, all must be welded into one by the Holy Spirit."[1]

Years ago I was watching a Billy Graham crusade. I was not listening very closely to the message until I heard him mention something about traveling through space. Well, that caught my attention! Dr. Graham proceeded to share some of his ideas about the afterlife. He postulated that, in our glorified bodies, we would be able to travel through space to visit other planets without the constraints of time and distance that limit us in our earthly bodies. He envisioned an infinite universe full of wonders waiting for us to explore and enjoy. Dr. Graham was imagining some of the things God *doesn't* reveal in the Bible.

I will be the first to admit that not all science fiction is appropriate entertainment for the believer, simply because much of it denies God and paints a hopeless picture of the future. But the books, movies, and television shows that I enjoy only spark my imagination and encourage me to welcome the limitless possibilities in God's wondrous creation.

My favorite science fiction stories involve what I call the "what if" scenarios. Most of these stories revolve around some type of time or inter-dimensional travel. The characters are presented with alternatives along the way that will impact the final outcome. One example of this type of science fiction is the Steven Spielberg trilogy, *Back to the Future*. The main character, Marty McFly, travels back in time from 1985 in a DeLorean time machine built by his scientist friend, Doc Brown. When Marty tampers with events in 1955, it completely changes the circumstances in his present. The two sequels to *Back to the Future* chronicle Marty's and Doc Brown's subsequent trips back and forth through time and their efforts to restore the space-time continuum!

One reason these scenarios appeal to me is because we are always being faced with choices. We know that every choice leads to a consequence. If we, as believers, recognize the potential impact of every choice we make, we are less likely to rush headlong into something without first considering the possible outcome. What's even more comforting, however, is the realization that *even when we make the wrong choice*, God's "time machine" of repentance and forgiveness is there to restore us.

The television show *Quantum Leap* is an example of the "what if" scenario from a different perspective entirely. If you have never seen this program, let me summarize its premise. A brilliant scientist named Sam Beckett theorizes that time travel is possible within one's own lifetime and develops the "quantum accelerator" to prove his theory. Dr. Beckett steps into the machine and finds that he has leaped into someone else's body in another time and place. It soon becomes obvious that he has lost control of the experiment. With the help of his holographic guide, Al, and an egocentric computer back home, Dr. Beckett leaps from one life to another, setting things right that once went wrong. Sam and Al realize along the way that **Someone Else** is controlling the "leaps" in order to restore people to their destinies.

Not everyone in my family finds science fiction as enjoyable as I do. I have tried over the last 30-plus years to acquaint Chuck with the value of science fiction as a valid means of escape from the chaos of reality. What I find refreshing and entertaining, however, frequently makes Chuck nervous. He does okay with movies or television shows that contain human-looking aliens, but the minute some strange "space creature" appears, he gets agitated. I have learned what he can tolerate and what he can't, and I appreciate the fact that what is enjoyable for me might border on torture for him!

Quantum Leap is one of the programs Chuck enjoys watching with me; another one is the long-running Sci-fi channel program, *Stargate SG-1*. This show, based on the feature film *Stargate*, revolves around a top-secret military installation called Stargate Command in Cheyenne Mountain, Colorado. Deep inside the mountain is an ancient device capable of transporting living and non-living matter to other planets instantaneously through a wormhole. The first time Chuck saw the wormhole generated by the Stargate, he got as excited as a child on Christmas morning.

"That's it," he exclaimed. "That's how we are supposed to connect to the heavenlies through worship—spiritual wormholes, portals to another dimension!"

Worship as Refuge

Of all the places of refuge available to us, worship is the one we can all share in common. As we release our fears, anxieties, distractions, and other cares of this world, we enter into a place of restoration. This restoration is what enables us to face a new day's challenges and chaos with renewed hope and strength.

Chuck co-authored a book with our worship leader, John Dickson, called *The Worship Warrior*. In Chapter five of this book, called "Portals of Glory," Chuck writes the following:

> Many of you reading this book are exhausted from all the strife, contention, and trials that have been linked to the promise that you have been pursuing. Stop and rest! That's what Jacob did. "Then he dreamed, and behold, a ladder was set up on the earth, and its top reached to heaven; and there the angels of God were ascending and descending on it" (Gen. 28:12). This was really a visitation from God.

In this visitation, God revealed to Jacob that He is the Lord of the past, the present, and the future. This brought Jacob into a relationship with the Lord. This caused him to have faith that he could actually grab hold of the promise and blessing that had been spoken over him. This also gave him confidence that he could have a relationship with holy God just as his father and grandfather (Isaac and Abraham) had.

From this experience, Jacob began to worship God personally in the following ways:

1. He acknowledged that the Lord had been in the place with him, even though before that point he could not see Him.

2. He memorialized the place, set up a stone and poured oil on it.

3. He renamed the place Bethel, the House of God.

4. He recognized God as provider.

5. He had a desire to give a portion of what he had back to the Lord.

6. The fear of God began to be a part of his life.

7. He declared that a "gate of heaven" had opened forever in that place. This would link his purpose on Earth into eternity.[2]

God revealed to Jacob that he could have access to Him through worship. He opened up a portal from earth to Heaven and ushered Jacob into His presence. As a result of his worship experience, Jacob was refreshed for the road ahead. He had been in the presence of Almighty God and was no longer bound by the chaos of his life.

We can experience the same renewal through worship. When we take advantage of our corporate and private opportunities to worship the King of Kings, the chaos and confusion of our lives recede. In the midst of our chaos, worship is an oasis of clarity and eternal reality that defies the wisdom of this world.

Endnotes

1. Oswald Chambers, *Oswald Chambers: The Best From All His Books* (Nashville, TN: Thomas Nelson, 1987), 172.

2. Chuck D. Pierce and John Dickson, *The Worship Warrior* (Ventura, CA: Regal Books, 2002), 82-83.

Chapter 10

THE PANTYHOSE SYNDROME:
ADJUSTING TO CHANGE AND DRESSING FOR FAVOR

To everything there is a season,
a time for every purpose under heaven:
…a time to gain, and a time to lose.
(Ecclesiastes 3:1,6)

M Y mother gave me my first pair of pantyhose in 1967 when I was 13 years old. At that time, I was five feet eight inches tall, weighed 115 pounds, and had no problem stretching that impossibly small bundle of nylon from my toes to my waist. Thirty-eight years later, however, a lot of things have changed. I mean, it's like the tensile strength of the nylon has increased to the point that I need hydraulics to stretch my pantyhose into position. I still scrunch up each nylon leg, carefully slide my feet into position, and inch the pantyhose up, but lately I have been running out of hose before the control top snaps into place.

Embracing Your Future Gracefully

I first noticed this problem in 2001, about a year after we moved back to Texas from Colorado. I had lost 15 pounds during our two-year sojourn in Colorado Springs, but after returning to Denton, the pounds slowly found their way home. We were all rushing around on a Sunday morning, getting ready for church, when I realized that something had gone very wrong with my wardrobe. Suddenly, everything I put on didn't fit, and my pantyhose refused to cooperate. By the time I managed to coax the last undamaged pair up to my waist, I was so exhausted and out of breath that I had to reapply my make-up.

As I stood in the middle of the bedroom gasping for air, my husband looked from me to the pile of discarded clothes and pantyhose and back again. He patted me on the shoulder and said, "It's okay, honey. I love you even with a little extra weight."

First of all, I can't stand to be patted. And second of all, I didn't want him to love me with a little extra weight. I wanted my clothes to fit again.

It's just not right. About the time you get comfortable in your own skin, your metabolism turns on you and your skin starts expanding. It's just not right.

Four years have passed since that day in 2001 when I first became aware of what I call "The Pantyhose Syndrome." You see, pantyhose are an excellent indicator of several aspects in a woman's life: size, flexibility, endurance, patience, to name a few. Men, unless they are figure skaters or ballet dancers, don't have the same reference. So, in a way, I suppose I should be thankful that my pantyhose opened my eyes to an increasing problem.

Maturity sneaks up on you. One day you are 25, full of plans and energy, able to eat a whole pizza with no consequences, and then, suddenly, your clothes don't fit anymore. You are walking down the street, minding your own business, when you catch a glimpse of yourself in a storefront window. Who is that woman that looks like my mother? Oh, no, it's me! Don't get me wrong—I'm still full of plans and energy, but I can't eat more than two pieces of pizza now without suffering the consequences.

For the sake of our mental, emotional, and spiritual health, we have to become reacquainted with ourselves as we grow up. When we leave childhood behind, we have to adjust to a new body and a new way of viewing ourselves and our surroundings. As we enter adulthood and say goodbye to the confusing days of youth, we breathe a sigh of relief and embrace a whole new world of responsibility and possibility. With the passage of time, we accumulate experience, wisdom, memories, and, hopefully, a sense of humor. Of course, some of us also accumulate several different sizes of blue jeans and a pile of reading glasses, but adaptation is vital to survival!

So, it's time to adapt to change…again. I must adjust to a new body and a new way of viewing myself and my surroundings, just like I did when I left childhood behind. And, thank God, this time I don't have to go back and be a teenager.

As I write this portion of the book, it is the last day of December. It's that day of the year when we typically reflect upon the previous 364 days and decide what to keep and what to toss in the new year. I am, by nature, a very practical person, so my list of things to toss every new year includes anything that I haven't needed or used within the last 12 months. Consequently, I spend several days every January cleaning out closets, drawers, and cabinets. As I discard or redistribute my accumulated items, I come face-to-face with those intangible things that have collected in my soul and also need to be eliminated.

I stopped using the words "New Year's Resolution" several years ago and adopted Daniel the Prophet's term: purpose in my heart. When Daniel was offered the rich delicacies of the king's table, he "purposed in his heart not to defile himself." And he didn't. When we purpose in our hearts rather than resolve in our minds to clean out, start over, or change in any area of our lives, something different happens. Our perspective changes when we allow our heart to overrule our brain.

A friend of mine told me she had an epiphany last week as she pondered her goals for the new year. Like me, she has reached that time in life when her metabolism decides to take a vacation. Normally, she vows every year to eat right, exercise, and lose weight, and every year she feels guilty when she fails. This time, the still, small voice of God said, "Seek me, and everything else will fall into place."

I was tempted to say that gravity has already made everything fall into unusual places, but I didn't. Instead, I looked into my friend's clear, green eyes and saw evidence of new hope. Buoyed up by her faith, I purposed in my heart to live one day at a time and enjoy the goodness of God in 2006 regardless of my dress size. Sure, it would be great if I could still eat anything I want and never have to think about the consequences, but those days are gone. I know myself well enough to acknowledge the fact that I enjoy good food and the company of family and friends too much to eat celery sticks.

As a woman of a "certain age," I have two viable choices when facing my current circumstances. I can regret the loss of my youth and make myself and everyone else miserable while I try to get back into smaller jeans; or I can rejoice in the fact that God has sustained me to the point in life when wisdom, experience, and a sense of humor make life so enjoyable. (There is a third choice, but it involves denial and eating everything in sight, so it's not a real option.) So, I will garden with renewed vigor, walk the dogs farther, skip second helpings (but not dessert), and seek the One who makes everything else fall into place.

I'll let you know how it turns out.

Being Reclothed for the Future

Sometimes it's difficult to embrace change; however, there are times when the Lord takes us through very peculiar circumstances and situations so we can understand that He is doing new things with us.

Let's continue with the theme of clothes and dressing. The Bible is filled with how our mantle is linked with our authority, and how our clothes are linked with our identity. Two of Chuck's dearest friends are Arlette and Lavon Revells of Georgia. Arlette is a beautiful, southern lady. They were at a leadership gathering once and she shared the following incredible testimony:

On June 8, 1985, I was awakened by a heavenly being. I was lying on my back and suddenly became aware of a larger-than-life body of white energy leaning over me. His hands were on my shoulders. "Get up," he said excitedly, "I have something special for you this morning." He vanished as I quickly slipped from under the covers, being careful not to awaken my dear husband, Lavon, sleeping beside me. I glanced at the clock. It was 4:23 A.M.

I tiptoed down the hall trying to keep the hardwood floors from creaking. I did not want to awaken our two children, Laura, who graduated from high school the night before, and Christopher, a tenth grader. Into the kitchen, Bible in hand, I sat at the table. I started leafing through the Bible. I didn't know what to expect or even what to do. Then, my mind heard these words: "From this day forward I shall supply your clothes my way. I will provide for all your needs. You shall be able to buy clothes for others, but I shall supply your clothes through others." (The first of three directives.)

I sat for a while, thinking about what I had heard. Disappointment took over. *Why was He so excited? I need a confirmation. I'll put out a fleece.*

"Lord, if this is really you telling me I can't buy my clothes anymore, please give me a confirmation dress today through someone."

That took care of it. Surely, if God was putting his finger on my clothes, He would answer my fleece!

Lavon and I had planned a pleasure trip to Helen, Georgia that day. All the way to Helen, I snuggled into my thoughts about what had happened. *Would I get my confirmation dress today?*

Expectancy took over. Strolling up and down the sidewalks in Helen I looked for a shop owner to lean out his door, look at me, and exclaim, "You're the one I'm to give this dress to." Surely there was a glow all over me. I had been in the presence of an angel! The day passed slowly as I walked in and out of shops. I didn't hear, "You're the one."

Late afternoon we started our 75-mile trip back to Athens. By then I was sure I had heard from God. On the way back I figured out how I would get the confirmation dress. Mother. She was helping at the church garage sale that day. I strained to see the dress hanging at the back door as we pulled into the garage. No dress.

It was getting close to bedtime. *No dress. Was it all just a dream? God, I don't understand?* Then, the still small voice spoke, "Your fleece was contrary to what I said. I will supply your clothes my way, and that includes my timing."

Thank you, Lord.

Not being able to buy more new clothes won't be so bad. My closet is full of beautiful things. I have probably got enough to wear the rest of my life if I *have to.* I loved silk dresses.

A few days later the second directive came: "I want you to give away every piece of clothing you have that you picked out."

"All right. Show me who to give them to." By then I knew something was going on and I wanted to be part of it.

I took an inventory of all my clothes. After going through everything, I found only two skirts and a blouse that had been given to me. Three things I had nothing to do with picking out! That would be my wardrobe. *But it would take a long, long time to give everything away, so I had a while... I thought.*

One evening something strange began to happen. It was time for my favorite dress to be prepared as a gift. I placed it in the washing machine in the laundry room. I looked down at my dress as tears poured down my cheeks. I felt like I was at a funeral. I peered into what seemed to be a casket and thought about the last time I had worn the dress and said my good-byes. This happened each time I prepared my offerings in the laundry room.

Nine days later I received my third directive. "As of today, you are to wear only what has been given to you." (I shared this with no one.)

I dressed for work that morning, putting on the blouse and one of the skirts. What was once too out-of-style to wear was now most precious. I looked in the mirror and said, "Thank you, Lord, for my clothes."

While preparing for dinner late that afternoon, I heard someone coming through the back door. I looked as my daughter, Laura, came into the kitchen, placed a beautiful package on the counter and said, "God asked me to buy this for you."

I quickly removed the ribbons and wrapping paper and lifted the top off the box. What should be nestled underneath the tissue paper but a beautiful pink silk dress. God's confirmation dress! Laura bought it with her first paycheck from her summer job.

This season lasted three and one-half years…and I never lacked for anything beautiful to wear.[1]

Seeing Ourselves Differently

Chuck and I have two different perspectives on clothing. My primary criteria where clothes are concerned is whether or not something is comfortable and can be laundered at home. Chuck, however, collects clothes like an art-lover collects paintings. His wardrobe is creative, changeable, and colorful, and almost everything he buys has to be dry cleaned! This can drive me crazy at times, but I have learned to appreciate our differences in so many areas that clothing is a minor bump in the road. I love him more than I love myself, which is why I gave him the extra closet all to himself. One reason he had to have the extra closet is because he has no problem alternating styles or sizes.

Chuck's creativity and confidence are reflected in the way he dresses. More than anyone I know, Chuck's self-worth is firmly seated in a vital, intimate relationship with the Lord. When he stands in front of the mirror, he wants to reflect the creativity and personality of his heavenly Father. If he shows up at church in a canary yellow sport coat and someone looks surprised by the color choice, it doesn't bother him at all. Chuck is confident of God's love and grace, and it shows in his clothes.

When I was feeling frustrated over the state of my shrinking wardrobe one time, he told me, "Listen, God loves me fat and he loves me skinny. He has revealed His love to me." That is one reason he has three closets full of clothes and I have one.

Of course, Chuck has a public ministry that requires him to dress appropriately. He also cleans out his closet regularly and gives armloads of clothes to others in need. I know of several men who browse through Chuck's closet instead of Foley's.

He believes the way we dress is sometimes linked with favor. While I could agree with him on this concept in principle, I wasn't sure how it operated in reality until one fall day in 2004.

Dressing for Favor

My son, Daniel, and his fiancée, Amber, were going with me to Home Depot. They were in the process of upgrading the interior and exterior lighting on Daniel's house before their December 18 wedding, and I had offered to purchase the fixtures for them. When they arrived at my house that Saturday morning in October, I was dressed in what Chuck affectionately calls my "uniform": blue jeans and a T-shirt. I was tying my shoes when Daniel and Amber came through the front door.

I dress for comfort whenever possible. There are times when I have to sacrifice that comfort and wear nice clothes and shoes, but the home improvement warehouse store is one place where I can walk in wearing paint-spattered clothes and not attract attention. In fact, I have been known to come straight from the yard, with mud-circles on my knees, to purchase more mulch at the garden center. So, blue jeans and a T-shirt would be the appropriate attire for this little outing.

As I brushed my teeth before leaving the bedroom, I glanced into the mirror. In that instant, I knew I was wearing the wrong shirt. It was a faded yellow T-shirt from Alaska that had been washed enough times to be truly comfortable, and there were no paint or mud stains on it anywhere. But still, it was the wrong shirt.

Do you ever experience those little moments of knowing that just make no sense to you? This was one of those times. I've been known to ignore those moments from time to time, but this time I didn't. I opened my closet door, peeled off the T-shirt, and donned an oversized red top Chuck had brought me from Nigeria. After tucking my shopping list into the shirt pocket, Daniel, Amber, and I were off to Home Depot.

I love going to Home Depot on a Saturday morning. All the weekend warriors are there, buying the tools and supplies they need for this Saturday's project, armed with the confidence that they can accomplish what they saw on HGTV or DIY network last week. As we walked through the main entrance and paused to look over the shopping list, the store manager approached me.

"Good morning," he said pleasantly. He spoke with a recognizable African accent. "Where did you get that shirt?"

I looked down at my shirt and said, "Oh, my husband brought this to me from Nigeria the last time he went there."

"And have you ever been to Africa yourself?" he asked with interest.

"No, I'm sorry to say, I haven't," I replied. "My husband travels extensively as a minister, and he always brings me something to wear!"

"Well," he smiled, handing me his business card, "I am from Cameroon, and just for wearing that shirt today, I want you to get ten percent off your purchases. Just present this card when you check out, alright?"

Of course, since I was getting a discount, I felt compelled to buy more than I had intended. After all, if I am going to get ten percent off my total purchase, then the more I buy, the bigger the discount. As we selected light fixtures and loaded them into the shopping cart, I thought back to that moment in my bedroom earlier that morning. Certainly, ten percent isn't a monumental discount, but had I ignored that gentle nudging about the yellow T-shirt and not changed clothes, I would have been paying full price for items I wanted to purchase anyway. Because I heeded that "little moment of knowing" back at the house, I had received favor from a store manager with fond memories of home.

What, exactly, does our apparel have to do with favor? According to First Samuel 16:7, *"...the Lord does not see as man sees; for man looks at the outward appearance, but the Lord looks at the heart."* The favor of the Lord doesn't depend on our outward appearance, so what was the Lord trying to tell me that day about favor? I'm sure Chuck would say that God wasn't too crazy about my "uniform" and was using a ten percent discount to get my attention, but I'm fairly certain that wasn't the point.

As a noun, Webster defines the word *favor* as follows: "friendly or kind regard; approval; liking; kind indulgence; permission; leave; unfair partiality." As a verb, the word *favor* is defined like this: "to support; advocate; be for; endorse; to make easier; help; assist." Anyone who has experienced the miracle of salvation can attest to the "kind regard" of the Lord Jesus Christ when He took our place on the cross. And yet, the favor of God extends beyond the extreme mercy of the cross to the continual support of our Advocate.

During the days following the death of our twins in 1988, I didn't feel particularly favored. I alternated between numbness, exhaustion, and resignation, yet I never doubted God's presence or wisdom in the midst of heartbreaking loss. One afternoon in early March, as I read my Bible and cried, the Lord illuminated Psalm 30:5 to me: *"For His anger is but for a moment; His favor is for life; weeping may endure for a night, but joy comes in the morning."* As I read those words I began to understand that the favor of God is not a magic formula for making life easy. Instead, the favor of God is the catalyst that turns darkness into light, despair into joy, death into life, and *"made my mountain stand strong"* (verse 7).

One of the great mysteries of our faith is the knowledge that we are "in Christ," clothed in His righteousness, which certainly has a lot to do with God's favor. No amount of window dressing will garner God's favor, because all of my efforts to clean up and look good are futile. Favor is like grace: I certainly didn't earn it, but I gladly receive it. God's favor is available to us because Jesus was obedient unto death, and we benefit from His sacrifice. In this spiritual family, the wayward siblings are covered by the goodness of the ultimate, unselfish Brother. Through Him, God's favor is available to all of us.

That day at Home Depot was a reminder that God's favor often hinges on our willingness to hear and obey the voice of God. A good father is patient with his children, generous with his favor, and tolerates mistakes and infractions up to a point. But there comes a time when the father has to hold the child accountable for repeated disobedience and carelessness. That's when the father begins to withhold his favor and allow the child to experience the consequences of his rebellion. Thankfully, as children of God, we have access to forgiveness and restoration, so we can return and enjoy the His wonderful favor.

Endnote

1. Arlette Revells, e-mail to author, March 28, 2002.

Chapter 11

PILLS AND BILLS:

FAITH, RESOURCES, AND RELATIONSHIP

WHEN our daughter, Rebekah, was just two years old, her favorite movie was the Walt Disney production of *Pollyanna* starring Hayley Mills. By the time Rebekah was three years old, she had memorized every line of dialogue in the film and could recreate her favorite scenes down to the smallest detail. She even found a thick, braided belt to use as a fake ponytail since her hair was too short to braid. Rebekah's obsession with *Pollyanna* meant that the rest of the family was subjected to repeated viewings of the movie, as well. Daniel would escape to his room or outside every time he heard the music begin, but John Mark was enlisted by his sister to help her play out the story over and over again.

One character in the story, Mrs. Snow, is an irritable invalid played by Agnes Moorehead. When Pollyanna first meets Mrs. Snow, she observes that the older woman doesn't look sick at all.

"Hmph," she responds indignantly. "Why, I'm right on death's doorstep. And the doctor—all he gives you is pills. Pills and bills, that's all."

"Pills and bills" became our favorite line from the entire movie. Anytime money was hard to come by around our house, Chuck and I would look at each other and sigh, "Pills and bills!" Even now, almost 20 years later, you will occasionally hear us laugh and say "pills and bills" as we try to balance the checkbook!

But for many of us, "pills and bills" is more than a funny line from a movie; it's a way of life. Whether it's the doctor bill, the grocery bill, the utility bill, or the housing bill, financial responsibilities can be overwhelming. There are times when bill paying can be like a lottery: lay out the statements, close your eyes, and pick one. Looks like the utility company gets paid this week!

Learn to Find Your Window of Opportunity!

When Rebekah was four, Daniel was seven, and John Mark had just turned three, Chuck went to Europe with an organization called Mission: Possible. It was springtime, and it had been two months since the death of the twins. The weather was glorious! The field in front of our house was full of Indian paintbrushes and bluebonnets, so the four of us went outside to enjoy the late afternoon sunshine. As the sun began to settle on the horizon, we all started back up the hill where we discovered that we had locked ourselves out of the house.

In 1988, when this took place, none of us had a cell phone in our back pocket, and the nearest phone was at the Piggly Wiggly down the street. With John Mark toddling along behind us, Rebekah, Daniel, and I worked our way around the house looking for an unlocked window. The last window we checked was the small one above the kitchen sink, and it was unlocked and open. It was also too small to accommodate Daniel or me.

I looked at my other two options. John Mark was a definite "no." Even if I could coax him through the window, he would probably just find food and go to his room to play. That left tiny, four-year-old Rebekah. She would fit, and she could follow instructions. The only problem was how could I convince her to do this?

In spite of being precocious and dramatic, Rebekah was full of fear at this stage in her life. The loss of the twins had affected her more than any of the other children, and she wasn't old enough to cope with all the emotions that loss had produced. As soon as I asked her to crawl through the open window and unlock the front door, her face registered raw fear.

"I can't, Mommy," she confessed. "It's dark in there, and I'll be all alone."

"But you can do it, I know you can," I encouraged.

I had almost given up and decided that we would all have to walk to Piggly Wiggly when I suddenly remembered our trip to Wal-Mart earlier that week. Rebekah had fallen in love with a new doll, but I had told her she would have to wait until we could afford it. She had sighed wistfully and left the doll on the shelf, but I knew she hadn't forgotten about it. After all, the doll looked just like Pollyanna's.

I took Rebekah's face in my hands and looked squarely into her big, blue eyes.

"Rebekah, if you will do this for me, I will take you to Wal-Mart tomorrow and buy that new doll for you." I was going to have to spend the money on a locksmith if she couldn't do it, so I thought it was worth a try.

In an instant, the fear on Rebekah's face was replaced with determination.

"Okay," she said. "I'll do it."

Within minutes Rebekah climbed through the window into the kitchen sink, lowered herself to the floor, and ran to the front door to let us into the house. After much rejoicing, Rebekah said, "When are we going to Wal-Mart?"

Provision is directly linked to faith. Rebekah didn't have the resources to buy that new doll even though she wanted it desperately. When I offered her a way to acquire the doll, she had to face her fear of darkness and isolation in order to do it. Her desire for the doll motivated her to activate her faith, overcome her fear, and receive the prize!

Fear is the great enemy of faith. How many times, when faced with a stack of bills, do we look first at our bank balance and then to the Lord? Jesus even had to remind His own disciples that God holds the world's purse strings in Luke 12:

> Therefore I say to you, do not worry about your life, what you will eat; nor about the body, what you will put on. Life is more than food, and the body is more than clothing. Consider the ravens, for they neither sow nor reap, which have neither storehouse nor barn; and God feeds them. Of how much more value are you than the birds?...Consider the lilies, how they grow; they neither toil nor spin; and yet I say to you, even Solomon in all his glory was not arrayed like one of these. If then God so clothes the grass, which today is in the field and tomorrow is thrown into the oven, how much more will He clothe you, O you of little faith?

Pass the Squash!

In the early years of our marriage, we lived in married-student housing at Texas A&M University in College Station, Texas. Chuck was going to school full-time, and I was working as a "stenographer" in the Texas Agricultural Extension Service Horticulture department on campus. Every month we used my little check to pay rent, buy groceries and gasoline, and purchase anything else we absolutely had to have. We discovered that we could buy TV dinners on sale and split them: I got the enchiladas, and Chuck got the rice and beans. Chuck lost a lot of weight during that time, but I had to keep my strength up for work, you know!

Whenever we could, we drove back to East Texas to visit family on the weekends. We could always depend on Chuck's mother, grandmother, aunts, and uncles to donate home grown vegetables and frozen meat to take back to A&M with us. One weekend we came back from Carthage with a cooler full of jars and freezer packages. As I unloaded the goodies into our refrigerator, I realized that every jar and package contained the same thing: *summer squash.* For the next month, I supplemented our TV dinners with squash cooked every imaginable way. (Did you know you can actually make pancakes with squash and a little flour?) As grateful as I was for the provision, to this day I don't eat summer squash unless it's the only choice.

There is no doubt that God uses our families as a source of provision in tight times. But even when the kindness of friends and family is not available, God will provide. As our pastor in Houston used to say, *"My Father owns the cattle on a thousand hills, so if I need help, He can sell a cow."* Over the years, our Father has "sold" a lot of cows, and I can truly say that *"I have not seen the righteous forsaken, nor his descendants begging bread"* (Ps. 37:25).

Pills: How Infirmity Works to Get Us Into Debt

Debt is an awful thing. I think if there is one thing that keeps our faith in bondage it is a debt structure working in our life. Debt is defined as something owed by one person to another person or an obligation or liability to pay or return something. In other words, you've gotten outside your boundaries in finances and you are now extended into a place that is creating a friction internally. That friction within you can even be a cause of many sicknesses.

Sicknesses can get us in debt—especially with all the medical costs at this time in history. We are hampered by rising insurance costs and that is being passed on to doctors who have been trained to help us understand what is happening in our bodies. Then there are the "specialty" doctors: you can go to the doctor for one thing and end up visiting seven more.

"Infirmity" is a term that encompasses more than just sickness and disease; it is also related to suffering and sorrow. Matthew 8:16-17 states that Jesus *"cast out the spirits with a word, and healed all who were sick, that it might be fulfilled which was spoken by Isaiah the prophet, saying: 'He Himself took our infirmities and bore our sicknesses'"* (see also Isa. 53:4). Infirmity can also refer to a disability of one kind or another. Infirmity can occur as a result of moral or spiritual defects that cause our will to stray from God. Infirmity can be related to the influence of an evil spirit (see Luke 13:11).

Infirmity can also be linked to an overall weakness in our bodies or to anything that created the weakness, such as grief. Romans 15:1 states that those *"who are strong ought to bear the weaknesses of those without strength"* (NASB). This weakness is infirmity. Not only did Christ bear our weaknesses and infirmities, but we are also called to bear the weaknesses and infirmities of our brothers and sisters in the Lord. This is called intercession. Romans 8:26 says, *"Likewise the Spirit also helpeth our infirmities: for we know not what we should pray for as we ought: but the Spirit itself maketh intercession for us with groanings which cannot be uttered"* (KJV). We have been called to intercede for the sick, which allows us to bring before the Lord someone weaker than ourselves.[1]

I Have to Press Through This Sickness

I (Chuck) am a warrior. I have had so many sicknesses that I have had to learn to war through them. I think the one story that really blesses me is the one of the woman with the spirit of infirmity who "pressed through" in Mark 5:25-34. She is an incredible example of personal overcoming. She overcame the religious structure of the day, the reproach of being a woman, and the stigma of being unclean. She pressed through to touch the Lord. This caused the Lord to release "virtue" (KJV; "power" in the NKJV) from His own body that healed her condition.

Jesus' treatment of disease was part of His redemptive plan of freedom. Jesus healed sick people. This was one of His major ministries. He dealt with many organic causes of illness and individuals affected by madness, birth defects and infections.[2]

We Do Need Doctors

I am not opposed to doctors. I would not be alive today without them. However, if you don't hear God in how to move with professional help you can spend all your money and end up owing them your future.

As is the case today, *prevention* was the most important dynamic of combating disease in Biblical times. It is interesting to note that based on our current understanding of disease, many of the laws that the Lord established in biblical times would have actually aided in preventing and combating various illnesses. Diet is one of the most important facets of health, which is why we find a number of laws relating to diet (see Lev. 11). Wine was also used to help stop problems and alleviate pain and discomfort (see 1 Tim. 5:23). We also find the use of ointments and salves in biblical times that were used for healing (see Isa. 1:6). James instructed the combined use of oil, confession of faults, and spiritual authority to produce healing (see Jas. 5:14).

In a world of chemical stimulation and overwhelming stress, it is a wonder that any of us remain healthy. Stress has such impact on our bodies—both physically and spiritually—that without the Lord as our strength, it would be impossible for us to live in this world. Jesus told us to be *in* the world, but not *of* it (see John 17:11, and 14). So why do we need doctors? One reason is because doctors are trained to understand dynamics *of* the world that can give us wisdom on how to be *in* the world.[3]

Bills: Do Not Let Poverty Keep You From Moving Into Your Future!

Have you ever been just overwhelmed with bills? I shared in an earlier chapter how I had to do the "one thing" that the Lord told me to do to break a cycle of owing too much money. Actually, if you remember that story, we began to experience healing as well.

One of the most dramatic times in our lives was when Pam found out she was pregnant with twins. This was one of the most jubilant and sorrowful times of our life. She carried both children to term, and then when they were born they were unable to survive in this world. We had lost two children, but the loss was compounded by another issue: The Lord had given Pam a word in 1979 that she would bear twins. The promise that had broken the power of barrenness that was holding Pam captive to endometriosis seemed to be lost along with the twins.

Not only did we have the loss of two children, but we also had huge medical expenses, funeral costs, and seemingly empty hands with no reward. But God!

Those two words—but God—have rescued my faith more times than I can count! And after years of giving to others, I watched giving break lose on our behalf. I had sown so many seeds throughout the years that God protected us from going into massive debt on top of experiencing heartbreaking loss.

My concept of money and debt was this: I always tried to stay within the boundaries for which I was responsible. This was good in a measure, but I was bound by it. While I thought it was such a high level of a faith walk, it was actually a degree of control and bondage. We had walked like this for probably seven full years in our lives. When Pam would tell me I wasn't really free in supply, I either didn't know or couldn't grasp what she was talking about.

All of a sudden, we owed thousands of dollars within a ten-day period of our lives. And of course, though many hospitals do have compassion over the loss that people experience, they still want their bills paid.

But God! Without me asking or saying anything, I watched people send gifts. I watched friends come to our aid. I watched family members (even those with whom we had breaches) call and express comfort and love. I believe the thing that touched me most was that the church to which we had belonged for 12 years in Houston rallied to our aid.

This was amazing since we had left that church two years earlier because of my missions call to closed countries. There wasn't a breach when we left this church, but we did experience some hurtful moments. It was a traditional church, and I chose to go with an organization that was non-traditional. However, this loss and their love overcame any religious breach that the enemy had tried to develop. One Wednesday night in their church service, when they announced our loss, they took up a large love offering and sent it to assist us in paying off our debt. The compassion of the people at the church had touched us and even brought us out of debt. But God! He had come through!

The greatest spirit that we seem to be contending with in our material society is the second cord in the braid of captivity: *poverty*. Poverty is refusing to become what God has created and destined us to be and not believing that the Lord can branch us into the fullness of His plan. Poverty is not just experiencing lack but also the fear that we will lack. Poverty occurs when we conform our circumstances to the blueprint that the world has surrounded us with. Poverty occurs when the god of this world surrounds and influences us with only a world perspective, causing us to forget God's ability in the midst of our circumstances. Poverty is the voice that says, "God is not able!"

Poverty can occur through various means. It can occur through oppression and wrong authoritative structures (see Isa. 5:8). It can occur if we develop a mentality of covetousness or gluttony (see Prov. 23:21), or are indolent or lazy (see Prov. 24:33-34). Haste leads to poverty (see Prov. 28:22), which occurs when we fall into "get rich quick" schemes. Poverty can occur if we resist the Holy Spirit and therefore negate the blessings of the Lord.

The main cause for poverty in our lives is failure to harvest. When we do not gather the harvest, a poverty mentality is set against us. Many times, the enemy will wait until our harvest time to develop strategies of devastation against us. Like the Midianites who always stole the harvest from the

Israelites (see Judg. 6), the enemy has already devised a plan to eat up our assets and returns.

We can plant. We can watch our crops grow. We can even have a time of harvest. *But if we do not take our opportunity to gather and steward the harvest, a strategy of poverty will begin to develop against us.* When we increase without developing the storehouses to contain what we have harvested, the enemy will gain access to our excess and to our future.

Other causes of poverty include aligning with structures that cause interest rates to go beyond a godly mentality of interest (see Neh. 5:1-5), fear and an unwillingness to face our enemy (see Prov. 22:13), and (succumbing to) persecution of faith (see 2 Cor. 6 and 8).[4]

GIVE Your Way Into Freedom From Pills and Bills!

Giving is a way of life for Pam and me. As a matter of fact, most people think I am motivated by prophecy because I am a Prophet. However, what motivates me is giving. God has shown me the power of seed time and harvest.

The issue of giving is probably one of the most controversial topics in the Body of Christ. Giving does not mean bringing a check or dollar to the church. Rather, giving is built around a covenant relationship that is linked around an altar of worship. Giving occurs when we recognize that *our King* is *righteous* and *legitimate*. We bless the Lord so that He will take His stand righteously on our behalf. Giving occurs when we worship! Giving occurs when we respond to authority with generosity and blessing. Giving occurs when we realize the lesser is blessed by the greater—that God is the Greater King and we should want to give all to Him. Giving occurs when we do not hold back what we have been entrusted with by the Lord![5]

Here are some things to remember about giving:

- He gave! He sent the expression of Himself through His Son as man. His Son gave His life for our freedom (see John 3:16).

- We should give because we recognize "MY KING is RIGHTEOUS and LEGITIMATE." When you give, only He can rise up over you in certain dimensions and serve as your judge. Only He can make you righteous.

- We give when we worship. Worship is an expression of faith in Someone greater than ourselves. Our being gives of its life back to its Creator when we worship.

- We give when we respond to authority with generosity and blessing. I love to give to those who cause my destiny to move forward.

- We give when we realize the lesser is blessed by the Greater.

- We give when we do not hold back what we have been entrusted with and over which we have stewardship.

Pills and bills and lions and tigers and bears, Oh my! I prefer to say, "BUT GOD!"

Endnotes

1. Chuck D. Pierce and Rebecca Wagner Sytsema, *God's Now Time For Your Life* (Ventura, CA: Regal Books, 2005), 96.

2. Ibid., 100.

3. Ibid., 101.

4. Ibid., 107-108.

5. Ibid., 112.

Chapter 12

PUT ON
YOUR SEAT BELT:
UNDERSTANDING BOUNDARIES
FOR OUR FUTURE

W HEN our children were little, we had lots of rules
designed to keep them safe and to prepare them for
their futures. They learned from an early age the "no-no's"
we all grew up with: don't touch the stove; don't cross the
street without a grown-up; don't hit your sister, and don't
walk behind the car when dad is in it. Of course, there were
special "no-no's" for each of our children that protected
them from particular dangers. For Daniel it was, "Don't forget to put the snake back in his aquarium." For Rebekah,
"Don't beat up any more little boys on the playground." For
John, "Don't bite!" For Isaac, "Don't climb any more brick
walls without a catcher," and for Ethan, "Don't get in
Dutch's face or he will bite you." (Dutch was our tempera-
mental dachshund, not a person.)

When Joseph turned 16, however, we had to develop a
new rule. This rule has remained the same as each of our
children has become a licensed driver. At this point, Ethan

is the last one at home without a license, but we have already initiated "the Rule" with him, too. And here it is: *Whenever you leave the house, let us know where you are at all times.*

Seems pretty simple, right? But you would be amazed at how many creative excuses a teenager can provide for why he or she didn't observe "the Rule" on a particular occasion: "I didn't have change for the pay phone;" "My cell phone died;" "John said he told you," or, my favorite, "I forgot." If there was a long list of rules to remember, I might consider "I forgot" as a valid excuse, but when there is only one rule, it doesn't qualify.

The beauty of this rule is that it keeps us parents informed of a child's whereabouts *and* protects the child from unauthorized, and therefore unprotected, activity. When Joseph was a newly licensed teenage driver, he asked to use the Volkswagen and take his girlfriend on a date. We gave him the keys and set his boundaries for that evening. Before he left on his date, Chuck reminded him, "Joseph, stay in the FM 1960 area and don't go into the city [Houston]. And remember, if anything changes or you are going to be coming home past your curfew time, call and let us know." He assured us that he would comply with our conditions and left to pick up his girlfriend.

You can probably guess where this story is headed. Joseph didn't stay in the FM 1960 area—he went into Houston and took his date to a restaurant inside the 610 Loop, a busy, congested commercial area. He didn't call us first because he knew we would veto the idea. He would have gotten away with moving outside of the prescribed boundaries, except for one thing: a friend of ours was eating at the same restaurant at the same time. (Don't you just love the Lord?) When the friend returned home, he called to talk and mentioned that he had seen Joseph and his date at the restaurant.

Fortunately for Joseph—or perhaps unfortunately—this was before the proliferation of cell phones, so Chuck couldn't call him and tell him to get home immediately. So Chuck waited up, and I went to bed. Actually, I didn't really want to be around when Joseph got home and found out that his infraction had been discovered!

Each of our children has learned, one-by-one, the wisdom and value of "*the Rule.*" Now that they all have cell phones, there really are no excuses not to notify one of us if plans change while they are out with friends. Most of the time, when one of them calls with a destination, activity, or time change, we approve it. Occasionally, however, calling first saves them from unnecessary and unpleasant consequences. Their boundaries are sometimes fixed, sometimes flexible, but always there for their protection.

Authorities Are Important

As our children grow beyond parental boundaries, they discover that other authority structures can impose rules on them as well. One such rule is the *seat belt law*.

Isaac is 16 and, like most boys his age, he knows more than his parents, local law enforcement, and the Supreme Court. A couple of months ago, Chuck was riding home from the bowling alley with Isaac. They had been having a good time with family and friends, and Chuck had left his car at the church office. When they were halfway home, Chuck looked at Isaac and noticed that he was not wearing his seat belt.

"Isaac," he scolded, "You aren't wearing your seat belt! Do you want to get a ticket and pay a $200 fine?"

"Man, Dad," he grunted, "can't we just have a good time without you telling me what I'm doing wrong?"

"Son, I'm just trying to keep you from getting a ticket."

Isaac grunted again, pulled over to the side of the road, and clicked his seat belt into place. Chuck told me when they got home that Isaac did not do this out of conviction for breaking a law, but just to shut him up. That night Chuck prayed an interesting prayer. He said, "Lord, I'm not going to strive this year over trying to convince people what is right and wrong. I am going to ask you that Isaac understand beyond the shadow of a doubt that You have put boundaries in place for his protection."

The next morning Isaac was meeting a bowling coach at Brunswick. He left the house in his car and headed across town. On the way, Isaac noticed that a white car was following him. He wasn't concerned because he was driving the speed limit and, besides, it wasn't a police car. He knew it was some official's car, but he really couldn't tell what type. When he recognized it was a Fire Marshal, he was confident that Fire Marshals did not give tickets.

He had almost reached his destination when the Fire Marshal flashed his lights and activated his siren to get Isaac's attention. After both cars stopped at the side of the road, the Fire Marshal approached Isaac's window.

"Do you know why I pulled you over, young man?" he asked.

"I think I do, but I don't want to say it," answered Isaac.

"I pulled you over because you aren't wearing a seat belt."

"Yeah, I thought that might be it."

As soon as Isaac finished at the bowling alley, he called his Dad to tell him that the Fire Marshal, not a policeman, had given him a ticket for not wearing a seat belt. Of course, Chuck acted surprised and said, "Really?!" And Isaac said, "I guess the Lord wanted to let me know that I was to wear my seat belt and obey the law." That meant that Isaac would be working extra hours in the ministry book room to pay the fine. There are always consequences when we violate a boundary!

Isaac is the first person I have ever known to get a ticket from the Fire Marshal, which made this incident even more unique. His brothers, of course, started teasing Isaac that the dog catcher was going to give him a ticket next time. So be sure and wear your seat belt!

Know Your Boundaries
and Get Ready for the Ride Ahead

We believe that many changes will abound in the earth in our lifetime, in our children's lifetime, and our children's children's lifetime. The Bible says:

> *Don't worry about the wicked. Don't envy those who do wrong. For like grass, they soon fade away. Like springtime flowers, they soon wither. Trust in the Lord and do good. Then you will live safely in the land and prosper. Take delight in the Lord, and He will give you your heart's desires. Commit everything you do to the Lord. Trust Him, and He will help you. He will make your innocence as clear as the dawn, and the justice of your cause will shine like the noonday sun. Be still in*

the presence of the Lord, and wait patiently for Him to act. Don't worry about evil people who prosper or fret about their wicked schemes" (Psalm 37:1-7, NLT).

Boundary is an important concept for an individual to learn. A boundary signifies a border or the entirety of a scope of something. A boundary is an imaginary line that creates a physical barrier. A boundary is also linked with legal rights. You have authority within certain defined limits. A boundary can also suggest the farthest extremity of a thing.

My (Chuck's) family had great potential for prosperity. That potential was never reached because my Dad could not understand the prescribed boundary linked with the prosperity that had come into his life. Therefore, corruption and many other issues invaded our lives, ultimately resulting in tragedy. My mother (Bernice) and grandmother instilled in me a tremendous understanding of the consequences of violating boundaries.

Pam's natural family was very similar. Both of her parents were alcoholics and lived outside the normally prescribed boundaries. This finally fractured her family. Thankfully, God had already prepared a place for Pam and her sister with their aunt and uncle in New Hampshire. Overnight, she went from a life devoid of boundaries to a life with a chief master sergeant in the Air Force as a father! Talk about change! Pam had to learn to observe and respect boundaries in a hurry.

David is an excellent biblical example of this principle. He usually stayed within His boundaries. The Bible says that David had "a heart after God." This is encouraging, because we know that if our heart is turned toward the Lord, then even when we make mistakes He can get us back on the right path with the right boundaries.

If you remember, David should have gone to war but he chose not to (see 2 Sam. 11). Sometimes even going to war can be the right assigned boundary for us. Instead, David went outside on his balcony. This seemed a lot nicer than the battlefield. But notice, because he wasn't at the right place at the right time, his emotions got outside of their boundaries. He saw beautiful Bathsheba bathing. Instead of warring, his passions were aroused and, before long, he had moved from lust to adultery to manipulation to murder. This led to, among other things, the loss of their newborn child. Makes you want to join the army if that is God's will for you!

Many people have a hard time with "church and religion." Structured religion can become very narrow in developing our mind-set of expression and worship. I believe we fall into issues of *law* rather than the *law of grace*.

The law is a boundary. The law was given to help human conduct remain in boundaries. Jesus came to fulfill the law. Man was created with a conscience. The conscience is like an "eye" that warns us or watches after us to protect us from getting outside prescribed boundaries. Most individuals do not understand that the Mosaic law was given as a temporary divine administration to help God's covenant people stay within their boundaries and protect them from sin and disease.

When Jesus came, He imparted the power of grace into the sin nature of man. Grace is linked with the privilege of aligning yourself with a person or relationship. Because of your love for that person and the relationship you have with them, you stay within the prescribed boundaries that will protect your relationship. The relationship that we have with the Lord Jesus Christ allows us to understand the best redeemed plan for our life in the earth. When He reveals His will to us in any situation, that actually becomes His "law" or "boundary" to us. When we experience His will, we experience His pleasure. He writes His word upon our heart. His rule is not an earthly rule, but a Kingdom rule that produces life within us.

God has put authority structures in our life to help us develop our conscience. He has given us His word. He has sent His Son. He is ruler of the universe. Yet He aligns our heart with His heart and thinking. He has given us a conscience so that we are not controlled by Him but we can respond to Him and prosper inside the boundaries He has given us. Once He tells you to do something, you just have to stay within those boundaries and you will prosper at what He has asked you to accomplish. These are all absolute authorities. All of mankind will have to understand this type of authority structure. Then there are also delegated authorities—leaders that are mentoring us, our employers, legal structures, and so on. All of these have been put in our life so we will fully understand His best plan for us.

Isaac had a boundary that he had to observe. It was simply: put on your seat belt. Psalm 104:9 says, *"And then you set a boundary for the seas so that they would never again cover the earth"* (TLB). Even the seas have their boundaries. In days ahead there will be great confusion, but we are protected in the prescribed boundaries that God has set for us. Put on the "seat belt" that God has for you, and that will help you make it to your destination.

Chapter 13

SOME MOUNTAINS YOU DO NOT WANT TO GO AROUND AGAIN:
TURNING UPWARD AND OUTWARD

As you can see, from an outward perspective, our life does not seem very simple. We've gone through many trying and testing times. Pam has raised our six kids (and many others to go along with them, as well as at least 20 pets). I believe trials and tests create testimonies. I hope some of the testimonies in this book have encouraged your faith so you can overcome and keep going, and actually end up better at the end than in the beginning. A testimony is built in a person's spirit. One of my very favorite verses that I have hung on to, meditated with, and really embraced as a life directive is Proverbs 18:14, *"The spirit of man will sustain him in sickness, but who can bear a broken spirit?"* If your spirit gets crushed through life's complexities and difficulties, you will find yourself depressed and weakened. Instead of facing life as an adventure each day, you actually give up and resign to just "making it through." You lose the joy and strength that should accompany our everyday existence.

This chapter has more of our life philosophy within it. Your belief system molds you and establishes your philosophy of life. I think you can tell by reading our book that the object of our faith is a Living God who sent His Son to obediently give us life. We both came into relationship with this Life Giving Man and God, Jesus Christ, through His eternal Holy Spirit that dwells in the earth. By His blood and an exchange of our sin for His covenant blessings, we have found peace, joy, and actually know that we have eternal life.

We also believe that we have a personal enemy. Satan is not some mythological figure. He has an organized government of evil in the earth realm and, believe it or not, targets each one of us because he knows we are all a threat to him if we align with the One who has already defeated His headship. He has a goal to vex our spirit. The word *vex* is linked with agitating, blocking, and stopping life from flowing freely from our inner being through our personality and affecting the atmosphere around us.

You Can Have a Sound Mind

Some of the most frequently discussed topics in our world today are linked with fragmented personalities. Most of us do not really understand that our spirit and mind labor together to express our life purpose. Today there is so much discussion on bipolar disorder, schizophrenia, and Disassociative Identity Disorder (DID). There is a rampant crisis with Attention Deficit Disorder (ADD) and Attention Deficit Hyperactive Disorder (ADHD). Really, it all boils down to this: *the enemy tries to separate and scatter our ability to "think straight."* He attempts to have us embrace fear—fear of the past overtaking us, fear of the reality of the present, and fear that we will never be capable of meeting the future. Second Timothy 1:6-7 says, *"Therefore I remind you to stir up the gift of God that is within you...."* In other words, keep the fires of your soul and spirit burning. Don't let the fire of passion go out. Verse 7 says, *"But God has not given us a spirit of fear but of power and of love and of a sound mind."* In other words, we have written that He can find your place of security, but this verse also says He can make you a safe thinker so you have disciplined thought patterns and, through self control, choose the best in life. A spirit of fear causes us to think incorrectly.

Don't Just Repeat Old Patterns Over and Over

The enemy has another plan: to get us going in cycles. He likes to get us so self-centered that we miss key cues from the Lifegiver over how to enter into and walk in joy and victory in the earth. One of my wife's favorite movies is *Groundhog Day. Groundhog Day* is about a weatherman who goes to see Punxsutawney Phil on Groundhog Day. If you have seen the movie, you will remember that Phil's cage is placed on an outdoor stage. When the time is right and the crowd is chanting, the groundhog comes out of his cage and is held up to the crowd. Then he whispers in the emcee's ear if he has seen his shadow. If he sees it, winter is extended. The real issue to understand here is that Phil has come out of hibernation to see if the season has changed.

In the movie *Groundhog Day*, released in 1993 and directed by Harold Ramis, Bill Murray plays a weatherman named Phil Collins who is covering the story of this weather forecasting woodchuck. What happens is that he begins to have the "worst day of his life" over and over again.

On the second morning of his visit, he awakens to find that Groundhog Day is repeating itself. This goes on for a very long time during which the weatherman comes face to face with the truth about himself: he is a selfish, cynical, lonely man with a predictably miserable life. Ultimately, however, Phil is given the opportunity to change everything as a result of reliving the same day! At first he uses Groundhog Day to improve his personal circumstances. (That is the way we usually respond when we realize that there is a better way—we want it to help us.) When one of the other characters in the story makes the suggestion that it could be a blessing to be able to relive the same day over and over again, he changes his attitude and begins to improve himself and consider other people. Really, he begins to see things he missed day after day!

He recognizes that he was living selfishly before, but as he relives each day he begins to realize he can improve or change the way he is living. He even begins to effect changes in others lives, as well. Therefore, he impacts everyone's life in the film.

Many of our lives are like this. We have to go around the same mountain several times before we recognize we don't want to go around it again. Many times we repeat the same mistakes over and over before we see there is a better way.

We Are in a Season of Breaking Cycles

Let me refresh you on what a cycle is. A cycle is an interval during which a recurring sequence of events happens. A cycle can also be a periodically repeated sequence of events, something that happens over and over at a certain time. Sometimes this is impregnated with supernatural phenomena. A cycle can be linked with time or event and orchestrated supernaturally so a repeating wound or injustice occurs from generation to generation. It is time for every old cycle that would bring you or your family decrease or destruction in the future to be broken in your life.

Pam has shared a lot of her life with you. Though her original family disintegrated, she was adopted by a wonderful Christian family that immediately began to discipline her and mold her for the future. My life was quite different from this. I had a very good family with great potential that was very established and then, the horror of all horrors, it disintegrated and we were scattered and left in disillusionment; lots of patterns and lots of cycles and lots of potential, but nothing moving right.

My dad had acquired the land linked with the previous two generations of his family members. He had done this through hard work. He was a very gifted man who married a very hardworking, determined lady. Together, they had all the ingredients for success. However, the enemy recognized this and found an inroad to attempt to destroy this family unit. His goal was to destroy the three generations that had connected. Actually, he went further than that and wanted to destroy the future generations—me, my siblings, and children to come. I could tell so many stories, but that would be another book! And some of the stories are so incredulous that it might better-suited to the fiction genre or a prime-time soap opera on television.

The point is that if we ever agree with cycles that have formed and choose to relive them over and over instead of life abundantly permeating the atmosphere around us, then death begins to have its dominion. Before long, we begin to be like the weatherman in *Groundhog Day*. We can't recognize our life purpose. We become selfish, cynical, lonely, and have a predictable miserable life. We tend to go around the mountain over and over again.

But God!

This is probably one of my favorite phrases. He can intervene and break these old cycles. Life and time are circular cycles. Even though we think linearly, we have to understand that in life processes God intended us to move through cycles: completing a cycle, passing on everything that we did well, and leaving those things that we did not finish to the next generation. He has a way to intervene and redo what has been lost or misappropriated. That is what He did in my life. At 18, He visited me for the first time, spoke to me, and said, "I can restore all you have lost." I wrote a book with Rebecca Wagner Sytsema on the power of restoration called *Possessing Your Inheritance*, and tell a lot of this story and share the principles of success and recovery.

However, this visitation became a process. Once you are visited and gain revelation, that word enters into your thinking process and breaks down all the old patterns that are holding you captive. Since that time I have had many visitations. When I was 26 the Lord visited me again, and this one changed the course of my life forever. In this time of interaction with a Living God, I questioned Romans 6:14 which says, "*For sin shall not have dominion over you, for you are not under law but under grace.*" I simply asked the Lord if this was true. We are talking about moving out of chaos and seeing the simple things of life. A lot of times we want a big explanation so we can understand every little "jot and tittle."

But the Lord simply said one word to me: "Yes!" I then asked Him if the whole Bible was true. He said three words: "Yes, obey it!" These words infused my body, soul, and spirit so completely that it reordered my life.

Actually, I had already read through the Bible several times since I was 18 years old. This time, however, the Lord had me read it in a different way. I felt the Spirit of God instruct me that I was not to read like I read a book or story, but I was to interact with every verse. In that interaction I was to embrace the truth of each verse. In other words, I could not go to the next verse until I told Him I believed the one I just read. That will really slow down your reading plan for the year! But it will also change the cycles of your life.

Breaking Old Cycles

I have already defined what cycles are. But there is a power that we can tap into that can cause any old cycle we have to change. We must remember that God has a remedy for iniquity. Hebrews 9:22 says, "… *without shedding of blood there is no remission* [of sin]." Remission means to send away or release from bondage or imprisonment. It means to dismiss what was so you can come out into a new expression. Without really understanding the shedding of Jesus Christ's blood there is no forgiveness of sins and breaking of old cycles. You have to remember a simple act of obedience that occurred for your life personally. Jesus went to the cross and died for you. Then He overcame death, hell, and the grave so you could live eternally.

Discipline also plays a real key in breaking old cycles. John 1:12 says, "*But as many as received Him to them He gave the right* [the authority] *to become children of God to those who believe in His name.*" A child goes through a lot of discipline. Sometimes I feel like we are never going to be trained up fully to get to where we need to be. But that is a promise also in the Bible: train up a child in the way he should go and he will not depart. Part of that training, though, many times has to do with entering spiritual discipline to break old cycles. You have to learn to pray. And many times you have to fast. Then there is the concept of spiritual work. You need to know that your assigned vocation is a major part of your discipline. How you relate to authority and understand the place you have been destined to be in is all part of your maturing in the Lord. In the midst of this we also learn that spiritual discipline called warfare—not with flesh and blood, but with the spiritual powers that are trying to keep us from exemplifying the Lord through our personality and accomplishing and receiving the best He has for us. Warfare is simply the conflict that it takes for you to find your abiding or dwelling place in the Lord. Once we start going through these spiritual disciplines and understanding truth, we go from victory to victory, glory to glory, strength to strength, and faith to faith. That sounds like a good cycle.

Now Is the Time to Turn Up and Outward!

There were so many mountains that became a part of our family life and inheritance. When the Lord spoke to me He began to show me how all of my valleys could be lifted up and my mountains could be made low and my path could be made straight. I love the Book of Deuteronomy. This is where Moses decides to reiterate the Law to the people because the time has come for an old cycle to break and for them to proceed again to their promise. He actually begins this earlier in the Book of Numbers. Here are some simple steps that will help you.

> *It is eleven days journey from Horeb by way of Mt. Seir to Kadesh Barnea. Now it came to pass in the 40th year in the eleventh month, on the first day of the month, that Moses spoke to the children of Israel according to all that the Lord had given him as commandments to them...and began to explain the Law saying, "the Lord our God has spoke to us in saying, 'you have dwelt long enough at this mountain. Turn and take your journey and go to the mountain of the Amorites...See, I have set the land before you; go in and possess the land....'"*

We must remember that after 430 years, the Lord had decided it was His time to break them out of the captivity in Egypt. He got them moving but they did not keep moving. Actually, if you keep reading Deuteronomy 1, you find that the people came up with a plan to go in and preview the Promised Land. Once they did that they saw the incredible promises the Lord had for them. But they also saw the war it would take to possess the promises. Therefore, remember, unbelief and fear became infectious in the camp and a cycle began that lasted 40 years. This is called a wilderness cycle. They were held wandering around in the wilderness and a whole generation did not go forth to possess all the riches and blessings that God was waiting to give. Now notice above, the Lord says, *"In the 40th year in the eleventh month, on the first day of the month."* God has a perfect time to break you out of old cycles. However, you have to just simply embrace what it takes to get out of those cycles. Here are some points:

There is a time to review your past. Review your journey and promises and accelerate (see Num. 33).

There is an appointed time to shift locations. You have gone around the same mountain long enough (see Deut. 1). Define the mountain you have been traveling around. Remember *Groundhog Day*. You have probably grown cynical going around this mountain. If you will open your eyes you can see how you can prosper in new ways. You will probably see others you have missed and how to bless them in their journey.

There is a time to take your next assignment. Take on your next war! (See Deuteronomy 1:7.) I find this really interesting. Notice what Moses says to them: To break this cycle we must go against the Amorites! There comes a time when you are willing to war what is keeping you from entering into the best that God has for you. They ran from the Amorites the first time. Now, 40 years later they would have to face them off to occupy the place of their blessing.

There is a consequence of not going forward and outward! Remember, if you decide to stay in a place and not move forward, you are going to reap what is in that place and all the atmospheric, environmental, and relational consequences of that place instead of the place of blessings God has planned for you.

Unlock Your Future Desire
and Let Your Spirit Rule Your Emotions

We talked about a spirit of fear earlier. Fear is a God-given emotion. But fear can also be a spirit. If we don't deal with our emotions properly (for instance, the emotion of fear) a spirit of fear will attach to our emotional well-being. The same thing goes with anger. Anger is a powerful emotion that needs to be expressed at times. However, there are ways that we should express this emotion of anger. If we do not express anger and deal with it in a timely manner, then that emotion will become a part of our personality. We will be known as an angry person. That is why in Ephesians 4:26, the Lord says, "*Be angry and do not sin: do not let the sun go down on your wrath.*" In other words, try to deal with anger before you go to bed so that you don't wake up with it embedded in your personality.

One of the keys to not going around the same old cycle is to get control of the function of *desire* within you. To desire is to long for, ask for, demand, or seek for what is most precious to us. Desire is linked with a *burning* to have something (see Gen. 3:1; Ps. 37). Remember, this is what deceived the woman in the Garden. The serpent conned her into believing that the Lord was withholding something from her that she needed.

Our praise and delight are linked with desire. One way that you can know you are treading around the same old mountain again is that you lose your desire to express praise and you are no longer experiencing the delight of life. Remember Elijah: *do not let weariness make you run from responsibility* (see 1 Kings 19).

I love the woman at the well. She did not let her past failures keep her from intimately worshiping and turning outward toward those around her (see John 4).

And finally, do not let past legalism and financial loss keep you from pressing through and gaining new power (see Matt. 9). The woman with the issue of blood, with little strength and no money, essentially said, "I am getting out of this mess and pressing past everything to touch the Lord."

To break old cycles you must find the boundaries to express your desires.

Unrestrained desires will lead to covetousness, presumption, dwindling vision, and decay! Review your boundaries and get your desires secured.

Give Your Way Into Victory!

I think the thing that made my life simple and brought me into victory was the discipline and joy of giving. What is giving? We first see the principle of giving when Abraham took the spoils of war and gave a tithe to Melchizedech. In Hebrews, we find that we are a Melchizedech priesthood that is being matured in God's plan in the earth. Giving occurs when you recognize "My King is righteous and legitimate!" There are many types of giving: alms, tithing, special offerings (memorial), and firstfruits. When you worship you GIVE! You give when you learn to respond to authority with generosity and blessing. Giving occurs when you realize the *lesser* is blessed by the *greater*! I guess the principle of giving I love the most is this: *True giving occurs when you do not hold back what you have been entrusted with as steward!* **Because He gave all!** I saw that this was my way into restoration.

The Lord began to teach Pam and me the principle of firstfruit giving. He revealed to us that He is the Firstborn over all creation (see Col. 1:13-16). The initial child born or crop produced is generally what is known as your *first fruit*. First means that which is preeminent in status or closest in relationship. Adam was the firstfruit of humanity, but Christ was the firstfruit of the Kingdom (see 1 Cor. 15:21-23). Therefore, Jesus has the greatest honor and is Supreme. The principle was this: When I learned to give the best of my first, He blessed my whole lump. If you want to know how He "restored all that I lost," it was from honoring Him with my first fruit.

You Are on the Verge of Completing a Major Season in Your Life. Do NOT Back UP!

Stake your claim! I love the book of Jeremiah. One of the principles of this book is that there is prosperity in the chaos of the world. Jeremiah prophesied this even in captivity. We must remember that God has a plan (see Jer. 29)! The Lord also revealed to us that His plan is good (see Jer. 31) and that there is a wonderful future in this plan. The greater promises are yet to come.

However, in this sequences of chapters, Jeremiah 32 displays that faith must take action. In the midst of Jeremiah's captivity, the Lord visits him and tells him to "buy a field." Jeremiah is in prison since he has prophesied that Jerusalem is going into captivity and is going to be destroyed. Now think about this. God tells him, "Go and buy the place that you just prophesied will be destroyed." This goes against Jeremiah's human reasoning. He first reminds himself that nothing is too hard for God. But he still attempts to convince himself that this is really what he should do. Many of us can so relate to this. We fully investigate and attempt to understand what we are to do instead of doing the one thing that we should do.

The Lord finally says to Jeremiah, "Is there anything too hard for Me?" It's one thing for you to think it, but another thing for God to say it! In other words, there has to come a time when your faith takes action and you stake your claim.

Finally, there comes that awesome wonderful promise: *"Call to Me and I will answer you and show you great and mighty things, fenced in and hidden, which you do not know (do not distinguish and recognize, have knowledge of and understand)"* (Jer. 33:3, AMP).

God has ways of showing you things that you do not know. That is why I don't embrace humanism. I know He has revealed over and over to me what I should do in chaotic situations. I think that is what has made my life more simple. I just try to hear and obey. Here are some things you can do to help you stay focused:

- Sit before the Lord and determine how He wants you to build for the future.

- Ask the Lord how your generation and life cycle connects with other generations.

- Ask Him to remove things from past generations that weakened instead of strengthened you.

- Ask Him how to pass on to the next generation those things that will bring them great victory.

- Define your alignments and assignments for the future.

- Don't take on every war or try and fix everything that is wrong.

- Don't try and connect with everyone in the world.

- Let God develop your connections and give you your assignments.

- **When you don't know what to do, "get your court seated."** This simply means: find those from whom you can get counsel.

- **Embrace His mind for increase and multiplication.** You have to think in a way that does not limit your ability to advance.

God Is Setting in Place His Order for the Future

Another thing that has always been key in my life is my prayer life. I learned early on that if I would order my prayers then He would order my day. If my day was ordered then my steps would be ordered. Order means this:

- To set in a straight row.

- A fixed or definite plan.

- Linked with law of arrangement and the sequencing of events.

- A state or condition in which everything is in its right place and functioning properly.

- A command, direction, or instruction.

- A request or commission.

Order is linked with every societal function we do, such as: architecture, finance, military, science, theology, politics, and even religion (for instance, grades of angels and rank of clergy). Order is the opposite of confusion. Therefore, we need to always seek God for His order!

Here are some mountains that we need to move. It is time to move from these mountains and turn outward into new victory. Stop and speak to these mountains in your life and say, "I am moving...

...from *Infirmity* to *Healing*,

...from *Poverty* to *Increase*,

...from *Religion* to *Accepting New Things*,

...from *Fear* to *Soundness*,

...from *Trauma* to *Peace*,

...from *Anger* to *Meekness*,

...from *Unforgiveness* to *Release*.

New Songs Break Old Cycles

I am telling you—there is a power in singing even if you don't sound good! There is something about the song of the Lord that breaks the power of the enemy. We find that in David's life when he would play on his harp and the demons that were influencing Saul would leave. To sing a new song doesn't just mean to sing a song that has never been. It can also mean to sing the right song at the right time. Old can become new. For instance, let me remind you of one verse of "A Mighty Fortress Is Our God."

And though this world, with devils filled,
should threaten to undo us,
we will not fear, for God hath willed

His truth to triumph through us.
The Prince of Darkness grim,
we tremble not for him;
his rage we can endure,
for lo, his doom is sure;
one little word shall fell him.

All of a sudden in a bad situation you remember this song. This song reminds you that just one little word can undo all the confusion around you. And also remember this: when God speaks to you, the responsibility to obey is yours. Many times your obedience will cause lots of problems for everybody else. However, it's not your responsibility to manage all the changes around you when you have simply obeyed. You are also not responsible for everybody else embracing your obedient revelation. Only you are responsible to embrace the change that is required of you. Once you do that, others associated with you can choose to allow their life to change based upon your obedience.

Then sometimes there are even radio songs that can really speak to you. There is a song that Tim McGraw sings that is called "Carry On." The song says this: *"What don't kill us makes us strong...carry on! You are never going to get anywhere running scared. If you will look down deep inside you will see what makes you strong. Carry on!"* I remembered to sing this one time while we were traveling. I also took this to a work/ministry associate of mine, Doris Wagner, when we were in a very hard, difficult time and we all sang it! Then there are those songs that just arise from your inner man. I call these songs of deliverance and freedom.

Receive Your New Mantle

Finally, the last thing I want to talk about is your new mantle. We wear the favor of God. We have talked a lot about clothing in some of the chapters. But let me remind you:

This is not a time for patching an old garment, but finding and wearing your new garment for your future (see Matt. 9).

This is a time to remove any old garment of death that represents your last season. Remember Lazarus. Jesus called him out of the tomb and removed all of his grave clothes (see John 11).

This is a time to receive new authority, reconcile any relationships (both good and bad) that would keep you from moving into what is ahead. And then follow hard to develop your new identity. Remember Elijah and Elisha. That was another garment issue (see 1 Kings 19:19-21).

This is also a time to receive the outfit that represents your new position and assignment. Remember Joseph. He lost garment after garment, but finally ended up changing his clothes and ruling Egypt (see Gen. 41:13-14).

This is a time to remove and put on. Let the Lord dress you for the future. One of my favorite passages is Zechariah 3. The Lord reminded satan that He knew all about the past of His people. However, He said, "This is My time to reclothe them and move them forward."

Awaken!

Don't sleep through the days ahead. Many times people sleep because they are depressed. Isaiah 60:1-2 (AMP) says:

"ARISE [from the depression and prostration in which circumstances have kept you—rise to a new life]! Shine (be radiant with the glory of the Lord), for your light has come, and the glory of the Lord has risen upon you! For behold, darkness shall cover the earth, and dense darkness [all] peoples, but the Lord shall arise upon you [O READER], and His glory shall be seen on you."

This is a time to awaken to our latter-day blessings even in the midst of our wanderings (see Hos. 6:1-3). This is a time for vision and provision for our future to be released. This is a time to MANIFEST a new bold identity. There is an anointing within you that is an inner oil and strength causing every old cycle in your life to let go. Let this inner "oil" come forth and get you through every narrow place. Let this inner life and strength of the Messiah reveal your best to you.

Epilogue

THERE WILL ALWAYS BE TROUBLED TIMES:
GRAB YOUR KEYS FOR VICTORY

Peace I leave with you, My peace I give to you;
not as the world gives do I give to you.
Let not your heart be troubled,
neither let it be afraid.
(John 14:27)

ONCE in a while, I abstain from the news. I don't read the newspaper or a news magazine; I stay away from the television during local and national news broadcasts, and I skip the news items on AOL and go straight to my e-mail. Since I am a stay-at-home wife and mother, this is an option that is available to me. My situation makes it possible to pull away from the outside world's chaos for a time. Of course, I know that I can't maintain my hermitage for long, so I enjoy my own personal chaos for a couple of days with no outside interference.

Inevitably, I have to return to that other place—you know, the one with headlines and sound bytes and news bulletins that screams things like, "Hamas Threatens Retaliation," or "Journalist Kidnapped," or "Unemployment Rate Soars." The headlines tell a grim story about a world full of hate, suffering, loss, and despair.

But we must remember the world is also a place that God loved enough to redeem from its chaos and desperation.

As mentioned in an earlier chapter, we know that bad things happen to good people—even God's people—and we are often caught up in whirlwinds, earthquakes, and fires over which we have no control. That's when we need, more than ever, to access the peace that only God can give and trust that we don't have to be troubled or afraid. After all, worry and fear won't change our circumstances for the better. In fact, they could actually make things worse.

Remember Romans 8:28-29? It says, *"And we know that all things work together for good to those who love God, to those who are the called according to His purpose. For whom He foreknew, He also predestined to be conformed to the image of His Son...."* That is, after all, the reason for the circumstances, no matter how small or large they might be. God is in the business of shaping us into the image of His Son, and the sometimes chaotic circumstances of this world make quite a workshop. Cooperating with Him is the best road through the confusion!

We have attempted to encourage you in writing this book. Our purpose was to communicate to you that even in the midst of the swirl around you, there is a simple thread of hope that can unravel the confusion and bring light into darkness. Find your boundaries and stand in the midst of those boundaries with a mind for victory. Face your trials with a perfect peace that passes all human, worldly understanding. Do not let the world determine your blueprint for thinking, but let the One who created you impart to you His best. He has a path. Let Him direct you.

Remember what Matthew 24:6-8 says:

> *And you will hear of wars and rumors of wars. See that you are not troubled; for all these things must come to pass, but the end is not yet. For nation will rise against nation, and kingdom against kingdom. And there will be famines, pestilences, and earthquakes in various places. All these are the beginning of sorrows.*

THE END IS NOT YET!
Bring Back the New Again!

In 1984, when I was eight months pregnant with Rebekah, Chuck and I attended a lay renewal weekend at our church in Houston. It had been a life-changing two days. Faith had been activated in so many areas of our lives, and everything felt new and fresh. As the weekend drew to a close, our pastor released the microphone and invited participants to share testimonies from the floor. Suddenly I was out of my chair and standing in front of the congregation, singing the words of a song made popular by Cynthia Clausen:

> *I can still remember the wonderful feeling*
> *Back when I first got to know You.*
> *It seemed the world was mine,*
> *I had joy, I had springtime.*
> *That's all just a memory anymore.*

Looks like I took my eyes off You, Lord.
But I don't want this callous feeling anymore.
Oh, please, bring back the way it was before!
Bring back the new again—I want to see You again!
Bring back the way it was when we began.
How did I miss the road?
When did I lose the glow?
And where did the wonder go?
Bring back the new again.

As soon as I sat back down, our pastor stood up and said, "Well, it's not over until the fat lady sings, so it looks like we're done!"

God had brought the "new" back into our lives that weekend by washing us in His word and increasing our faith for the journey. We faced the future with new hope and determination, confident that our Father was in complete control.

Here are some points from Chuck to help you "set your face like a flint" to enter into your future with a mind for victory:

1. **Instead of allowing the Storms of Life to over-whelm, advance as a violent praising STORM throughout your life ahead.** May praise arise in you as you enter your future.

2. **Do not fear the enemies of this world.** Remember the Prophet Elisha saw into the heav-enly realm and saw more angels waiting to come to his aid than the enemies that were surround-ing him to capture his life. Ask the One who loves

you most to uncover any *plots of the enemy that are forming against you and yours*! Do not let the enemy defeat you or create a focus of anguish for you through mishaps, disappointments and circumstances. ***See the BEST that is there for you and go for it!***

3. **Be disciplined to meditate on Life-giving principles and not the chaotic news reports of the day.** Meditation is the key to success and victory. Protect your "eye and ear gates." The words that enter you take root and will produce fruit.

4. **Do not be afraid to FAST.** Set aside three days every quarter to deny yourself of the thing that could be keeping you from stepping into your victory. Before you enter any major repositioning or change in your life, fast for three days to disconnect from anything in the past that would try to defeat your future. Fasting is a spiritual discipline that sanctifies and disconnects you from structures that would hinder your progress. If you do not understand this discipline, Arthur Wallis's book, *God's Chosen Fast*, is a wonderful tool to assist you.

5. **Watch for BREACHES!** Life is full of repositioning and changing relationships. Do not let the enemy cause broken relationships as you move forward in your changes. This is a time to expect an amazing turn of events. Learn how to forgive. Learn how not to take up offenses. Learn how to bless your enemies.

6. **Ask for a new EXPECTATION in life.** Expectation is linked with hope and is a function of our

emotional being. Expect change! Look at issues that have gone before you and expect a 180-degree turnaround! Decree that this is a time of reversal of fortune. Counteract your Faith Destroyers. The enemy will not remove your faith, but attempt to make your faith empty.

7. **Break Old Cycles!** Let me refresh you on what a cycle is. A cycle is an interval during which a recurring sequence of events happens. A cycle can also be a periodically repeated sequence of events, something that happens over and over at a certain time. Sometimes this is impregnated with supernatural phenomena. A cycle can be linked with a time or event and orchestrated supernaturally so a repeating wound or injustice occurs from generation to generation. I am praying that every old cycle that would bring you or your family decrease or destruction in the future is being broken in your life. I am declaring that you enter into God's restorative power.

8. **Believe that you can be RESTORED!** Restoration is the power of returning to any place where "God's best covenant plan was deviated from." Restoration includes reclaiming lost land, lost health, and lost joy. Restoration is linked with restitution. For instance, if a stone in your house was broken by a workman, it is substituted with another that is even better. I am declaring that every broken stone in your foundation will be replaced with new strength in the coming year. Restoration also means the perfecting, mending or fitting together of every detail of your life that will cause you to complete or end your race

greater than how you began it. If the enemy tried to overtake you in the past, I am decreeing that you have new strength to outrun him and finish stronger in your Future. May God **UNRAVEL every old cycle in your life linked with a three-fold cord of poverty, infirmity and religion**.

- The opposite of **poverty** is *increase* and *trust*.

- The opposite of **infirmity** is *healing* and *strength* through joy.

- The opposite of **religion** is being willing to *embrace something new* when presented to you.

This is a time to *pray that what has been lost in past seasons and not recovered will be found. Thank Him for your times of discipline and days of preparation.* They will be compensated with FAVOR! For every place of victory attained and every old cycle broken, expect a new mantle of favor and joy to be placed on you. Let Him become your rearguard, *so the path ahead is secured for you.*

There is still One who speaks to us today. I hear Him saying: "*Let Me rearrange your circumstances. Look deep in every circumstance around you for they are setting a new order for your life. Let Me remove your past. Do not strive to hear Me. Let your prayer life be one of asking in simple faith and I will answer you. I will release favor so you can build your future. Let Me train your hands to prosper for building. Stake your claim on your future and expect Me to do wondrous things on your behalf this year.*"

Signs in the earth are being revealed to us so we will understand that times and seasons have changed. **Learn to think NOW!** Let your *INTUITION* be activated. *BREAK the* *power of OBSESSION* by knowing that you cannot control everything in your life. *REMOVE anxiety, fear, doubt, anger, frustration, guilt, jealousy, and envy*. Get ready to *EMBRACE many changes* in your life. *REDEVELOP* your way of *communication (first in prayer with your Creator, then with each other)*. Quit striving and let faith develop. Faith occurs when we enter into God's rest. Most people think rest is where we pull aside and do nothing. Rest actually means that you cross over and enter into your "promised destiny." You are being prepared to enter in.

This is not a time to strive or manipulate circumstances in order to try to see God's will manifested in our lives and the things for which we are praying. As a matter of fact, Jeremiah 33:3 says, *"Call to Me and I will answer you and show you great and mighty things, fenced in and hidden, which you do not know (do not distinguish and recognize, have knowledge of and understand)"* (AMP). I believe if we just cry out to the Lord and watch carefully then we will see Him rearrange circumstances and bring supernatural revelation into our life. I am watching this happen. Don't strive as you pray for your children this year. Don't strive over your job. Ask God for wisdom; He will release to you what you are to say and do at any given moment. He will use others divinely on your behalf. He will penetrate your cells and mind during the night through dreams and visions.

Yes, this is a time to be WATCHFUL! To watch means to look out, to peer into the distance, to investigate or get a new scope on something, to see an approaching danger (see 2 Kings 9:17-18) and WARN those endangered, to review and evaluate your household (see Prov. 31:27), or to SEE so you can GUARD your FUTURE.

Your path is FORWARD and not BACKWARD! This is a time where we must allow God to show us the future so we can advance. Time is not linear the way we think. Time is in the form of a circle. Therefore, if we move toward our future, God will restore our past. He will also order our path so that we reconcile everything that would be a hindrance to what He has ahead for us.

Learn to rule in the midst of your "Babylon" or the world around you will try to overtake you! When I say Babylon, I am talking about the world and religious system that aligns together. Babylon will attempt to make you submit emotionally, bodily, and intellectually. Babylon will also use a combination of persecution and seducing worldly mind-sets to cause you to submit to its blueprint. Be like Daniel! Do not let dainties tempt; do not let lions produce fear; do not let other leaders cause you to change your spiritual focus; do not let visitation overwhelm you. Babylon has captured so many of us in the past. Rule in the midst of your Babylon!

Finally, do not take yourself so seriously that you lose the ability to laugh. Laughter is the best medicine. Joy is our strength. Learn to laugh not only with your friends and families but at the enemies around you that attempt to defeat you. When we do this, we will see that *in a world of chaos, we will not miss the simple things*.

Blessings and joy,
Chuck and Pam Pierce

CONTACT INFORMATION

GLORY OF ZION INTERNATIONAL MINISTRIES

CHUCK D. PIERCE

P.O. BOX 1601

DENTON, TX 76202

FAX: (940) 565-9264

WEB: www.glory-of-zion.org

NOTES

Additional copies of this book and other book titles from DESTINY IMAGE are available at your local bookstore.

Call toll free: 1-800-722-6774.

Send a request for a catalog to:

Destiny Image₀ Publishers, Inc.
P.O. Box 310
Shippensburg, PA 17257-0310

*"Speaking to the Purposes of God for this
Generation and for the Generations to Come."*

**For a complete list of our titles,
visit us at www.destinyimage.com**